Marriage
and Family Building
in Islam

Dr. Muhammad Abdul Bari

Ta-Ha Publishers Ltd.
www

© Copyright **Ta-Ha Publishers Ltd.** 1427/January 2007

Reprinted June 2010

Published By:
Ta-Ha Publishers Ltd.
Unit 4, The Windsor Centre
Windsor Grove
West Norwood
London, SE27 9NT
website: www.taha.co.uk
email: sales@taha.co.uk

Written by: Dr. Muhammad Abdul Bari
Edited Dr. Abia Afsar-Siddiqui and Abdassamad Clarke

A catalogue record of this book is available from the British Library

ISBN-13: 978 1 842000 83 0

Printed and bound in the UK by
De-Luxe Printers Ltd.,
London NW10 7NR

Cover/Book design and typeset by Shakir Cadir, shakir@iways.co.uk

In the name of Allah,
The Most Gracious, The Most Merciful

Marriage is part of my sunnah,
whoever runs away from my path
is not from among us.
(Sahih al-Bukhari)

Table of Contents

Acknowledgements

This book is the outcome of my long involvement with youth and community work in Britain. Many people, including the very young and old, have contributed to the ideas contained in it. They all deserve my sincere thanks. The decision to write it was taken when I was running the 'Islamic Perspective of Parenting' course with an Internet-based virtual organisation, 'Witness Pioneer' in 2000. Since then it has been running almost every year. I am indebted to them for giving me the opportunity.

I express my deep appreciation for the contribution of my wife, Sayeda, for her understanding, support and contribution in writing the book. In spite of the pressure of life, her excellent family management and sense of humour continually encouraged me to sit at the computer. I am grateful to our four children, Rima, Raiyan, Labib and Adib for their enthusiasm during the process of writing. May Allah reward all of them with the best of rewards.

I am grateful to Dr. Hasan Shaheed, Rumman Ahmed, Ruqaiyyah Waris Maqsood and Dr. Jameel Qureshi for their valuable comments on the first draft. I am also indebted to a number of

'*Ulama* of the Islamic Forum Europe for helping me in finding references from the Qur'an and books of *hadith*.

May Allah shower His blessings on all of them.

Dr. Muhammad Abdul Bari
Dhu'l Hijjah 1427 AH
January 2007 CE

Introduction

With the increasing complexity of modern life Muslim families face many challenges. For Muslims living in modern societies, keeping the family unit intact and raising children in Islam are becoming daunting prospects. Although there are exemplary features in the Muslim community regarding family bonding and child rearing, unfortunately many Muslims do not seem well-equipped to withstand the storm of secular and materialistic ideas regarding man-woman relationships, marriage, family and other aspects of life.

Present day Muslims all over the world are simply struggling to cope in the midst of this transformation of values. Many of them live in the past and find pleasure in roving through their lost glories of intellectual discourse and creative thinking. While 'traditionalists' tend to put their heads in the sand in order to escape from the future, 'secularists' want to abandon many Islamic values at the altar of 'modernism'. Some are imprisoned in the mindset of the colonial legacy. Muslims are at an historical juncture. The post-September 11th world has brought new challenges and opportunities for us.

We know for sure that, over past centuries, things have gone terribly wrong for Muslims in many directions, including our family life. The immense pull of *jahiliyah*, and the general ignorance, complacency and indifference among the Muslim masses are disturbing. Family breakdown and various social ills that have gripped other communities are now engulfing Muslims. Unless addressed openly and robustly, this could bring psychological alienation in our children leading to social disaffection and spiritual emptiness. In fact this is already beginning to happen and unless dealt with, will lead to a crisis for the Muslim community.

The encouraging thing is that there is now a positive realisation in many quarters of the Muslim community of the need to work vigorously to build our future. It depends on how Muslims can best stand up to the challenges of modern materialistic life and address the issue of fortifying families to anchor our children in the positive ethos of Islam. If Muslims want to safeguard their Islamic identity, build their families and communities and work for the common good of humanity, building families and raising children in Islam should be brought to the forefront of our agenda. Conscientious members of the Muslim community should join hands with the positive forces in the wider society to start a broader pro-family movement.

The purpose of this book is, first, to raise awareness among Muslims about the ever-increasing importance of marriage as the only acceptable human relationship for sexual fulfilment and human continuity. It discusses different aspects of marriage, how and when it should be done and important issues, such as marital breakdown, divorce procedures, forced marriage and polygamy. Secondly, it discusses the family as an historic institution, the features and purposes of Muslim families, the rights and responsibilities of family members, and important issues related to the family, such as extended families, domestic violence and fostering. The modern threat to the family and family values, the basic ingredients needed to make a blessed family, the ethos and principles of Muslim families, and the impediments that can cause family disharmony – all these have also been tackled briefly.

The family is the cradle of human civilisation. It is the centre for nurturing human beings, the emissaries of Allah on earth, preparing them to take on the generational task of sustaining stable societies. Family is the first nursery, and the school and university that produce a nation and civilisation. Although formal schools, community and governance play their vital role in nation building, they will surely fail if families fail in their job. A happy family environment is the best thing parents can give their children. Any parent who feels passionately about raising children properly should care first about building a sound family.

The book is written for ordinary Muslims who have a sense of urgency for their community's future and who want to do something about it. Human life is complex and as such there could be many approaches to addressing an issue, depending on cultural or other factors. Unless specified in the *Shari'ah*, any opinion in the book should be taken in that light and should not be taken as judgmental. The book is an educational and social one. Although broad Islamic principles are highlighted, it is not meant to be a book of *fiqh*. I have followed the broad Islamic principle that anything not forbidden in Islam is generally acceptable. This book is an attempt to regenerate Muslim communities in the modern world. I rely on the forgiveness of Allah for my shortcomings and pray that He accept this humble work.

NOTES

Translations of Qur'anic verses are based upon The Meaning of the Glorious Qur'an by Mohammed Marmaduke Pickthall and The Noble Qur'an by Abdalhaqq and Aisha Bewley.

It is established practice among Muslims to mention the supplication ﷺ – peace and blessings be upon him – after the Prophet Muhammad's name and this will be the practice here. In the same manner, other Prophets' names are followed by ﷺ – peace be upon him – and companions' of the Prophet Muhammad ﷺ names are followed by ﷺ / ﷺ – may Allah be pleased be with him/her.

CHAPTER ONE

The Institution of Marriage

**And We have created you
in pairs.**
(Qur'an 78:8)

**And of His signs is this:
He created spouses for you
of your own kind so that you
might find tranquillity in them.
And He has placed affection
and mercy between you.**
(Qur'an 30:21)

1.1 THE SIGNIFICANCE OF MARRIAGE IN ISLAM

Allah has created everything in pairs and bestowed an inherent physical and emotional attraction between members of the opposite sex.

The attraction towards and sexual desire for the opposite sex are part of human nature and develop during puberty, the transformation from childhood to adolescence. The Islamic way of life leads young people toward lawful marriage that satisfies sexual, emotional and social needs in a secure and loving environment. In permissive societies, teenage romances, encouraged by societal and peer pressures, involve illicit physical relationships, often between socially and psychologically immature boys and girls. The result is obviously disastrous and both the social and economic price that a society pays as a result of legalising pre-marital sex, is high. Children as young as twelve are reported to be parents of unwanted babies and the high percentage of teenage pregnancies outside of marriage has become a societal norm. Even the heightened campaigns for 'safer sex', with condoms as the panacea, are failing to halt the rise of this social burden. On the contrary, this 'condom culture' is destroying the fabric of society; religious and spiritual values are looked down upon or sidelined and marriage as a social institution is losing both its importance and its sanctity.

It is a natural part of adolescence to explore new boundaries and embark upon adventurous pursuits independently. At this age, the sexual urge, being new, exciting and powerful, can cause young people to lose focus in their lives and lose sight of their priorities. Uncontrolled and irresponsible sexual relationships can ruin the future of youngsters and expectation of a normal life.

Marriage is a social contract between two human beings of the opposite sex. It is also an institution that encompasses the joy of human relationship between a man and a woman. Since the beginning of human history, men and women have been bonded in marriage in order to procreate, thus ensuring the continuity of the human race. Throughout history, marriages have given rise to families that formed tribes and races, societies and nations and this will continue to be the case until the end of time, regardless of the passing fads of liberalism, materialism and atheism. Since ancient times, it has been a social practice and reflects the character and customs of that society. Marriage is performed through a contractual procedure, normally based on revealed law, and is in many religions and cultures, inviolable. It is the union not only of two individuals but of two families and indeed marriages have influenced war and peace at various times throughout history.

Marriage is fundamental to the existence of human beings on earth. As well as providing solace, comfort and pleasure between two people, marriage teaches them the value of compromise and sacrifice in order to live happily together. It is an institution that unites a man and a woman in mutual relationship, affection and trust, thus providing the ideal conditions for nurturing the next generation. Until very recently, marriage between a man and a woman has, throughout the world, provided the legal validation of children's social acceptance and legitimacy to inherit from their parents. Like other revealed religions, Islam views marriage as the only acceptable outlet for a sexual relationship and the only basis for procreation. The most important right of children is that they should be born within a stable and loving home. They must not be the fruits of passing lust between a man and woman outside marriage. Adultery and fornication (*zina*) are two of the gravest wrong actions in almost all religions including Islam and their punishment is severe. As a result, marriage occupies a most important step in a Muslim's life. Allah has prescribed marriage as the main way for a conjugal relationship and starting a family (see Qur'an 2:221, 5:5, 24:32-33). According to the Prophet Muhammad ﷺ, marriage is 'half of the *deen*'.

> *When a slave of Allah marries, he completes half his deen, and he must have taqwa of Allah to complete the second half.* (Al-Bayhaqi)

Allah has blessed marriage with many benefits including:
- the legal fulfilment of sexual desire within a secure relationship
- peace of mind and tranquillity
- increase in service to Allah
- reward for fulfilling one's duties towards the family
- the joys of children

Sound family life teaches the importance of love, care, responsibility and affection. Inevitably, difficulties will arise in any human relationship and these need to be handled with sensitivity and compassion. The marriage bond, if conducted within the bounds of Islam, encourages the development of faith, spirituality and social values among the partners and the arrival or existence of children only works to further cement this bond.

In Islam, husbands and wives are described as 'garments' (*libas*) to each other (Qur'an 2:187), a unique and most apt comparison that describes the complementary nature of the man-woman relationship on earth. Spouses, like garments, serve to protect each other from the outside world, to adorn and beautify each other (i.e. to bring out the best in each other), to provide comfort and support to each other, and this is true for both husbands and wives.

Marriage is a lifelong commitment that needs much hard work from both parties to ensure its happy, long-term survival. Mutual love, affection and *sakinah* – tranquillity – that come after the wedding are very deep-rooted and powerful emotions unlike the superficial feelings of lust and physical attraction. Real love between a husband and wife is a very beautiful blessing of Allah and can be eternal, even after death, if both husband and wife strive within the boundaries of Islam. The love and affection of the Prophet ﷺ for his wives, particularly *Umm al-Mu'minin* Khadijah ﷺ and A'ishah ﷺ, to mention two jewels of the Prophetic household, is a role model for all time to come and a reminder to those who think that married life is dull.

In some societies, not long ago, marriage was encouraged in order to produce more children so that they would become 'productive members of society'. While in agricultural societies, this still remains so, marriage in developed countries is seen as a 'trap' or a burden that limits individual freedoms. The Prophet Muhammad ﷺ has asked Muslims to marry at an appropriate age and lead a balanced life on earth. He also advised Muslims to have children so that his *ummah* becomes large in number on the Day of Judgement. Celibacy, unless for some unavoidable reasons, is not encouraged in Islam, as the Prophet ﷺ said:

> *Marriage is from my sunnah. Marry women who are beloved and loving and bear children, because I shall be proud of my ummah on the Day of Judgement.* (Abu Dawud and an-Nasa'i)

A group of three men came to the houses of the wives of the Prophet ﷺ asking how he worshipped Allah, and they were informed about that. They considered their worship insufficient and said, "Where are we from the Prophet ﷺ as his past and future wrong actions have been forgiven?" Then one of them said, "I will offer the prayer throughout the night forever." The other said, "I will fast throughout the year and will not break my fast." The third said, "I will keep away from women and not marry them ever." Allah's Messenger ﷺ came to them and said, "Are you the same people who said so-and-so? By Allah, I am more submissive to Allah and more afraid of him; yet I fast and break my fast, I sleep and also marry women. So, he who does not follow my sunnah is not from me (not one of my followers)."
(Sahih al-Bukhari)

Islam is opposed to selfishness and greed. Infanticide, abortion and avoiding or delaying having children just for fear of poverty is hateful in Islam and is unbecoming of human dignity.

Do not kill your children out of fear of being poor. We will provide for them and you. Killing them is a terrible mistake. (Qur'an 17:31)

1.2 ARRANGING MARRIAGE

In an Islamic marriage, the consent and choice of both the boy and the girl are paramount. However, families from both sides can be involved in advising young people in their choice in the light of their experience. In this context, marriage in Islam is often broadly an arranged or assisted affair. In Muslim culture, every relevant person in the family contributes to building a new family. The family and society all have stakes in the success of a Muslim marriage. Parents, relatives and friends often help in their own ways to find marriage partners for their loved ones. Mature boys and girls are themselves allowed to choose their life partners provided that they adhere to the norms and decencies of Islam. Coerced or forced marriage is not acceptable in Islam. In fact, no marriage is valid without the consent of the boy and the girl themselves.

Islam has clear and well-defined laws for the interaction between men and women. Dating, clubbing and 'free mixing' of the sexes are considered unacceptable. Muslim men and women have been asked to follow the Qur'anic command of lowering their gaze when they encounter the opposite sex:

> **Say to the believing men that they should lower their eyes and guard their private parts. That is purer for them. Allah is aware of what they do. Say to the believing women that they should lower their eyes and guard their private parts and not display their adornments, except for what normally shows...** (Qur'an 24:30-31).

Thus, courting before marriage is not allowed in Islam. Pre-marital 'boyfriend-girlfriend' relationships for fun and romance, or indeed for any reason, are alien to Muslim culture. Cohabitation or 'living together' is a grave wrong action in Islam.

In an environment where young men and women study and work together, it is not unlikely that 'innocent love' or a natural liking may develop between two young Muslims. While many parents may wish to ignore this issue, wise parents need to be open with their children and advise them on how to remain within the boundaries of Islam. If, in this type of situation, parents realise that marriage is the only solution they should arrange it without any delay. Young Muslims should be taught from an early age and reminded thereafter, that men and women who are not closely related (*mahram*) should not meet each other in seclusion.

> *Whenever a man sits with a woman in privacy, a third one always creeps in, and that is shaytan.* (At-Tirmidhi)

Decent interaction for valid reasons, for example, education and learning purposes, between a man and woman in the presence of others is different from this. It is important for both sexes in these situations to conduct themselves with individual piety. This is something that must be instilled in children from a young age. It is not something that can be enforced by law when the children have grown up.

The purpose of this apparently 'strict' segregation of men and women is to uphold high standards of moral conduct and decency within society and to prevent people from acting on passing whims and desires that will be of no benefit to them as individuals and to society at large. A society in which the individuals do not adhere to the guidelines given by Allah, will inevitably find itself degenerating into chaos.

Choosing a Marriage Partner

Marriage in Islam is by means of a proposal, and both parties should give priority to *taqwa*, good character and compatibility (*kufu'*). A couple having little in common, in terms of essential qualities, will find it difficult to hold together for long. The Prophet Muhammad ﷺ was a pragmatic leader, and on one occasion he advised Fatima bint Qays, a female companion, to marry Usamah ibn Zayd, the son of his freed slave and fostered son, instead of one of two other companions, Mu'awiyah or Abu Jahm, because of his concern for their compatibility (Sahih Muslim). Truthful, honest and believing men and women look for similar qualities in their partners. On the other hand, partners with baser qualities will naturally cling to each other:

> **Corrupt women are for corrupt men and corrupt men are for corrupt women, good women are for good men and good men are for good women.** (Qur'an 24:26)

Choosing a marriage partner is a challenging job.[1] Marriage is about bonding two hearts and is thus dependent on Allah's blessings. For a successful marriage, both partners need to satisfy each other regarding the issues they feel important, no matter how trivial they seem to be. Family background, personality traits, habits, attitude and manners are all important. Although no marriage can succeed without the spirit of compromise, the major issues need to be sorted out before a match is finalised. Women probably need more assurance on some aspects of men, even though a Muslim society may have the support mechanism.

In Islam there is no concept of unnatural social strata and this is also true when it comes to the marriage of two Muslims. Caste systems have been created by human beings and derive from the days of ignorance or the ancient caste systems in some communities,

---

1. *Bent Rib: A Journey through Women's Issues in Islam* by Huda al-Khattab, p15, Ta-Ha Publishers, London, 1997

but this concept is alien in Islam. However, what is encouraged in Islam is a genuine 'compatibility' and 'wisdom'[2] for a social, intellectual, economic and educational match between two partners in marriage. Compatibility in age is also an important factor. Although, on occasion, the Prophet Muhammad ﷺ encouraged a male companion to marry virgin girls, there should not be any stigma in marrying widows, because he himself married widows. He advised Muslims not to marry only for the sake of beauty, as desire for beauty often brings moral decline. He also advised not to marry only for the sake of wealth, as wealth often becomes the reason for disobedience to Allah. He asked Muslim men to look for *taqwa* in their prospective partners in order to ensure a sound Islamic upbringing for the future generation. Beauty and wealth are extra blessings, but should not form the only criteria for a life partner. According to *hadith*:

> *A woman is married for four things: her wealth, her beauty, her lineage or her deen. Always choose a woman for her deen.* (Sahih al-Bukhari, Muslim, Abu Dawud and an-Nasa'i)

> *This world is all temporary conveniences, and the greatest joy in this life is a right-acting wife.* (Muslim)

Marriage provides soothing comfort to the life partners. Allah has naturally bestowed on women the greater share of mercy, love and compassion. Men, on the other hand, are bestowed with strong will and assertive and adventurous natures. For a man to succeed in marriage his intellectual maturity and accommodative quality are vitally important.

---

2. *The Family Structure in Islam* by Hammudah Abd al-Ati, pp94-97, American Trust Publication, 1977

Muslims, both men and women, are advised to supplicate for Allah's guidance (*istikharah*) while choosing a marriage partner:

None fails who consults (others) and none regrets who seeks (the Creator's) choice. (At-Tabarani)

Below is a list of some prominent features to look for and major questions to ask potential husbands and wives. The list is not exhaustive. One cannot expect wholly positive features in one's potential partner or 'perfect' answers to all questions. Marriage is a compromise and people should reflect upon their own strengths and weaknesses in order to be realistic in life.

1.3 WHEN TO MARRY

When should a Muslim marry? The answer lies in the *sunnah* of the Prophet ﷺ. Islam prefers marriage at the appropriate age, i.e. when a boy or girl becomes physically, emotionally and intellectually mature, and is fit to take up the social and economic responsibilities that marriage brings. A man must enjoy some level of economic sustainability in order to maintain a family.

Marriage is a joyful event and there are many advantages to marrying young. The youthful couple can play with each other and with their children so as to enjoy the pleasures of life in a *halal* way. For lively engagement with the children, early marriage helps youthful parents to face the challenges of rearing young ones. Marriage is a conscious commitment to a life-partner for a future family role, and a serious job that affects both partners, the children, and the community as a whole. The earlier that young

Table 2.1 – Important qualities to look for in potential husbands and wives

Husband	Wife
❧ Understanding and commitment to Islam	❧ Understanding and commitment to Islam
❧ Honesty, integrity and reliability	❧ Honesty, integrity and reliability
❧ Social and life skills relevant to men	❧ Social and life skills relevant to women
❧ Sacrifice and ability to accommodate	❧ Sacrifice and ability to accommodate
❧ Education and professional expertise (primarily to earn for family)	❧ Education and professional expertise (primarily to raise children in Islam)
❧ Family background	❧ Family background
❧ Strength of character as in the role of a provider and protector in the family	❧ Loyalty to husband in goodness
❧ Positive outlook, magnanimity and broad-mindedness	❧ Liveliness
❧ Ability to cope with anger, crises and external pressure	❧ Interest and skills in household chores
❧ Competence and enthusiasm to lead a family in Islamic ethos	❧ Feminine qualities, eg tenderness and care
❧ Willingness to consult	❧ Ability to cope with domestic pressure and the demands of children
❧ Equity, impartiality and sense of justice	
❧ Masculine features, eg toughness and stamina	

Table 2.2 – Suggested list of major questions to ask a potential partner

Husband	Wife
❧ Is he medically sound?	❧ Is she medically sound?
❧ Does his family have any bad history?	❧ Does her family have any bad history?
❧ Does he understand women's rights in Islam and is he ready to accept them in this case?	❧ Does she understand a husband's rights in Islam and is she ready to accept them in this case?
❧ Is he stingy in financial affairs?	❧ What are her views on having children and how to rear them?
❧ Does he easily become angry and does he blame others for this?	❧ Is she a feminist or individualist?
❧ Does he have any bad habits, eg smoking?	❧ Does she have a basic knowledge of Islam and does she understand its broader message?
❧ Is he self-centred?	❧ Is she a balanced individual?
❧ Does he have a basic knowledge of Islam and does he understand its broader message?	❧ Is she interested/involved in community service (*khidmah*)?
❧ Is he a balanced individual?	
❧ Is he interested/involved in community service (*khidmah*)?	

people are exposed to these realities, the easier it will be for them to adapt and adjust to married life.

It is not necessary for a young man to have a high income in order to start a family. A *halal* income that can support the couple with dignity is the basic requirement. This is something that young people need to start thinking about during their school years and exploring from an early age the available opportunities that will provide both a *halal* income and will fulfil the young person's potential and talents. It is imperative they increase their professionalism and skills through education and hard work, so that they can live with dignity and become active partners in society.

> *The first thing of the human body to purify is the abdomen, so he who can eat nothing but good food (halal and lawfully earned) should do so…* (Sahih al-Bukhari)

> *The flesh that is nurtured with haram wealth cannot enter the Garden. The Fire is his abode.* (Musnad al-Bari)

In Islam, earning to support his dependants is primarily the man's responsibility. He has been burdened with this role since the beginning of human creation. But seeking knowledge is compulsory for both men and women in Islam. Illiteracy and ignorance among women is disastrous for the family and for society as a whole. Islamic history is filled with pioneering Muslim women who contributed to the *ummah* in many areas of life. Women in other cultures, for example, Florence Nightingale and Emily Pankhurst in Britain, were pioneers in establishing the rights of women in their days.

However, Islam has not placed the responsibility of earning and supporting dependants on women. This is the sole responsibility of a man. The wife has a right, according to *Shari'ah*, in the earnings of her husband, but the husband has no right over the earnings of his wife. Thus, it is inappropriate for Muslim women with young children to go outside the home to earn without valid reason at the expense of raising their children. Young children need the security of their mothers and if they are absent for long periods then this has a negative effect in the formative period of young children and at the same time puts extra pressure on them. An exception to this would be if the family is in hardship and an extra income is needed. As the children become more independent, there is no reason why women should not earn if they wish to, provided that the home is not neglected and that the working environment is a *halal* one. It is worth mentioning at this point that rearing children is not the sole responsibility of the mother and that fathers should also spend quality time with their children and ensure that they too do not spend long periods away from home.

The 'right time' to get married is very much linked to a conscious understanding of Islam and *tawakkul* (reliance on Allah), not merely on good earnings. Young Muslims should not wait for an 'ideal time', as it will probably never come in anybody's life.

In many societies where promiscuous relationships have become the norm and marriage is losing its sanctity, Muslim boys and girls should leave no stone unturned in preparing themselves for early marriage so that the allurements of the opposite sex cannot drive their passion into un-Islamic acts. Khalif Umar ﷺ said, "Two things prevent marriage – inability and being a wrong-doer." Of course, the decision to marry is a big step for a young person, and conscientious parents should play an active role in encouraging their mature son or daughter to marry early. If for some genuine reason there is delay in marrying, young men and women should follow the Prophet's ﷺ *sunnah* of fasting.

> *The Prophet ﷺ said, "O young men! Whoever among you is able to marry, should marry and whoever is not able should fast regularly, as this will be a shield for him."* (Sahih al-Bukhari and Muslim)

1.4 THE MARRIAGE: A SIMPLE OCCASION

Marriage is a happy occasion and the contract is public so that the relevant people from both the bride and the groom's sides can participate in the joy. The Prophet Muhammad ﷺ instructed Muslims to announce marriages publicly and arrange a feast according to their financial capacity.

The marriage ceremony or *Nikah* itself is very simple and has the following essential requirements:[3]
- the consent of the bride and groom
- consent of the bride's guardian (*wali*)
- the presence of two Muslim witnesses
- agreement on the groom's *mahr* (dower) for the bride

The marriage contract takes the form of 'offer' and 'acceptance'. One party, usually the guardian of the bride, expresses the offer (*ijab*) of marriage according to specified terms and the other party expresses their acceptance (*qubul*) of the bride according to the terms specified. Any knowledgeable Muslim male can officiate

3. *Raising Children in Islam,* Suhaib Hasan, pp18-22, Qur'an Society, London, 1998

over the marriage; there is no concept of clergy or priesthood in Islam. It is also recommended at this time for the marriage official to deliver a marriage sermon or *khutbah an-nikah* and end the *nikah* with a *du'a* for the newly married couple.

The giving of the *mahr* (marriage-gift or dower) by the groom to the bride is a Qur'anic injunction:

> **And give the women (on marriage) their dower as a free gift...** (Qur'an 4:4)

It may be payable in any form such as cash, property or it can be a service rendered. There are numerous examples during the time of the Prophet Muhammad ﷺ which illustrate that dowers ranged from dinars to iron rings to teaching the bride a portion of the Qur'an. There is no specified minimum or maximum as far the dower is concerned but it is recommended that moderation is exercised. *Mahr* can be either paid at the time of the *nikah* (*muajjal*) or it can be deferred (*muakhkhar*) or a combination of both.

After the consummation of the marriage, it is *sunnah* for the groom to hold a wedding banquet or *walima*. This should not be a lavish or expensive affair but a simple one to which family, friends and neighbours, rich and poor are all invited, according to the Prophet ﷺ:

> *The best wedding is that upon which the least trouble and expense is bestowed.* (Mishkat)

> *The worst of the feasts are those marriage feasts to which the rich are invited and the poor are left out.* (Mishkat)

Unfortunately, due to outside cultural influences, marriage in many Muslim communities has been marred by practices unacceptable in Islam. The simplicity prescribed by Islam is gradually being replaced by inessential social customs.

For example, there is a trend for the bride's family to ask for a high *mahr* in order to maintain a 'social prestige'. The consequences of this are many. Young men in some countries are finding that they cannot marry at an appropriate age simply because they cannot afford to do so. Some men, after accepting the condition of a high *mahr*, then do not pay it, either in whole or part, thus depriving the woman of her Allah-given right. Islam has prohibited such *mahr* as is beyond a bridegroom's capacity.

In some communities, there is a custom in which the groom's family demands cash or household goods from the bride's family. This is absolutely against Islamic practice as it is the groom's responsibility to provide for his wife. There is no dowry system in Islam (the giving of a marriage gift from the bride to the groom) only the dower (*mahr*) in moderation which is given from the groom to the bride.

Even the simple Islamic marriage feast has turned into a string of several expensive and pompous functions, with unnecessary superficialities and *haram* actions taking place such as free-mixing and pop music and mixed dancing. There can be no *barakah* in a marriage that is conducted in such an un-Islamic way.

1.5 OTHER IMPORTANT ISSUES IN MARRIAGE

Marrying a Non-Muslim

Allah has permitted Muslim men to marry women from *Ahl al-Kitab* (People of the Book, i.e. Jews and Christians). However, some Muslim men have not truly understood this point and have married women who have little adherence to their own religions. What is the success rate of these marriages? How are the children raised, in terms of their religion and culture, in these dual-faith families? To be fair, the situation is generally disappointing. Apart from some exceptions, where the Muslim men have strong roots in Islam, many of these marriages either end in mutual recrimination or create situations where the children become the casualties. They grow up with torn identities and confusion in their lives. Young Muslim men should keep the following Qur'anic verse in mind, when marrying a woman from the People of the Book:

Made lawful to you on this day are... (in marriage) chaste women from the believers and chaste women from those who were given the Scripture before you.
(Qur'an 5:5)

Young Muslim men would be well-advised to consider the long-term effects of such marriages over their short-term desires. The product of marriage, children, are assets for any human society, which is why some Muslim scholars have advised that such marriages should only be practised in Muslim lands where the environment for rearing children in Islam is positive. Khalif Umar ﷺ discouraged believing men from marrying outside Islam during his caliphate, fearing that Muslim men might leave Muslim women unmarried. This is an important issue a Muslim cannot take lightly.

Muslim women, on the other hand, are categorically prohibited from marrying non-Muslim men under any circumstances. Occasionally, due to the heavy secular influences in some Muslim families, a few Muslim women are marrying non-Muslim men. However small the number may be, this sad state of affairs is the sign of decline. A young Muslim woman raised in Islam would have attempted to invite the man to Islam before marriage. Islam should take precedence over any worldly desire.

Polygamy

Polygamy is a misunderstood topic that evokes excited debate in the non-Muslim world. The fact is that Islam does allow polygamy, albeit with restrictions and conditions and for good reasons. However, throughout the *ummah* today, monogamy is the norm, while polygamy is the exception. Why and when Muslim men are allowed to practise polygamy is a major topic.

Polygamy was normal practice among Semitic and other peoples throughout history and many people around the world do still practise it for various reasons. In Islam polygamy is quite specific and is for men only. It is acknowledged that there are some difficulties associated with such a family set-up; women may find it psychologically difficult to 'share' their husbands, thus creating some family tensions, while men may find it difficult to maintain 'justice' among wives. But there are situations when polygamy is the only recourse that brings welfare to society. The Qur'an has clearly outlined the conditions when a man can enter into polygamy and limited the number of wives at any one time to four:

> **If you are afraid of not behaving justly towards orphans,**
> **then marry other permissible women, two, three or**

four. But if you are afraid of not treating them equally, then only one… (Qur'an 4:3)

This *ayah* was revealed after the Battle of Uhud when the Muslim community was left with many widows and orphans and a deficit of men. In order to ensure that all women could enjoy the comforts of married life, this *ayah* was revealed. It does not give men the license to marry many women for their own desire or self-interest for which women suffer. Anyone fearing Allah will not abuse this law.

Polygamy in Islam ensures that men give women their rights as wives and any resultant offspring are legitimate. Its permissibility saves society from men having numerous mistresses without marital rights or children that are unrecognised within the legal system. Allah has set as the limit four wives at any one time so that marriage does not become a farce. This is the just decision by the Creator of both men and women.

Forced Marriage

The practice of forced marriage has been known to occur in some sections of the Muslim community. In some cases, girls are taken to the country of their origin by their parents and forcibly given in marriage to their kin. In other cases, girls may be 'tricked' into marriage, often to wholly unsuitable people, for economic or immigration reasons.

Whatever the circumstances that lead to this cruel and unjust practice, the root cause of this is usually the ignorance of the parents regarding the laws of Islam. Despite loving their children and wanting the best for them, these parents may have a misplaced sense of duty, a faulty interpretation of family honour and a complete lack of communication with their children. But the damage is far-reaching, not only for the young people themselves, who will inevitably rebel against their family, their community and their religion, but for the image of Islam in those countries where these appalling acts are occurring.

Islam has nothing to do with forced, or even coerced, marriage. The Prophet of Islam ﷺ annulled at least one marriage which was conducted forcibly and which the woman did not accept.

> *If a man gives his daughter in marriage in spite of her disagreement, such a marriage is invalid.* (Sahih al-Bukhari)

> *A young woman called Khansa bint Khidam once came to the Prophet ﷺ complaining that her father wished to force her to marry her cousin. The Prophet ﷺ told her that she had the right to reject her father's choice. But Khansa replied, "I accept my father's choice, but I wished to let the people know that our guardians cannot force us in marriage."* (Ahmad, Ibn Majah and an-Nasa'i)

While a woman cannot be forced to marry someone against her wishes, she needs to have the approval of her guardian in order for the marriage to be valid. The Prophet Muhammad ﷺ said:

> *"A woman's marriage without the consent of her guardian is void."* (Ahmad)

Therefore, it seems that a balance needs to be struck between the wishes of the young people themselves and their parents. This is where a good upbringing and plenty of open communication are essential.

Same-sex Partnerships

Like the two other Abrahamic faiths, Islam is unequivocal that marriage is only between a man and woman. Marriage, or the voluntary and exclusive union of a man and a woman as husband and wife, is a religious requirement. 'Marriages' or partnerships between people of the same-sex are categorically forbidden and there is no compromise on this in Islam.

Muslim parents should be clear in their own understanding on this and educate their children from Islamic principles. They should also be aware that their children may be exposed to media which may promote libertine sexual practices and attitudes, and work to limit this exposure as far as possible. Same-sex relationships are damaging to the divine institution of marriage and to society as a whole.

1.6 MARITAL BREAKDOWN

It is a sad fact that despite the many benefits that marriage can bring to both partners, it can end in tears. There may be a number of reasons for this:

- loss of physical and emotional love and warmth between husband and wife
- unrealistic expectations from each other
- rudeness and abuse from husband or wife
- mistrust between them
- unwanted intrusions of family members
- infertility and impotence
- infidelity
- mental illness

- departure from an Islamic way of life by one or both of the partners

Entering into a marriage is always a gamble, but there are steps that can be taken to ease the transition into married life. Like any other human organisation, family members have complementary roles in order to make it work. Young people need to be aware of their respective roles and responsibilities within marriage before embarking on this journey. Many young people have unrealistic romantic notions about married life, unrealistic expectations of their partners and generally a lack of awareness about the hard work and sacrifice that marriage entails. Tolerance and compromise are the key qualities that are required. It is unbecoming for a Muslim to behave rashly and in haste for patience and forgiveness are great virtues. Islam has provided guidance about every sphere of daily life and marriage is no exception. By working to seek the pleasure of Allah and acting within his commands, there is a greater chance that a marriage will be successful.

When marital difficulties do arise the couple has to think seriously and work hard to stay together and this should involve plenty of open communication with each other, either alone or in the presence of an experienced and understanding elder.

Islam advocates *sabr* – steadfastness – and as such divorce should not be carried out in haste. It is a painful process and needs a great deal of reflection and mature consideration. Both partners should have enough time and space to think objectively about its implications. Can they reconcile on their own? What sorts of sacrifices are needed to mend their differences? How much can a member of the family or someone closer help in this? One has to weigh up all the positive and negative factors in taking this serious decision, especially if there are children involved.

If every sensible effort fails and divorce becomes inevitable this should be done amicably, before the relationship becomes too bitter. Islam has saved husbands and wives from the 'better dead than divorced' situation. Marriage in Islam is not life imprisonment.

Islam has allowed *talaq* or *khul'*[4] – two types of divorce, one for men and the other for women – on genuine grounds. In fact there is a whole chapter on the subject in the Qur'an, Surat at-Talaq. However, it should be borne in mind that divorce is the most disliked of those things that are acceptable in Islam.

> *Prophet Muhammad* ﷺ *said, "Of all things permitted by law, divorce is the most disliked by Allah."* (Sunan Abu Dawud)

There has been much misunderstanding with regards to Islamic divorce, although this is a simple procedure which is clearly outlined in the Qur'an (see Qur'an 2:226-237). Islamic procedures are to be followed strictly[5] if the couple want to please Allah. *Talaq* occurs when a man decides to divorce his wife according to the appropriate guidelines. When a woman wants divorce from her husband she has to undergo a process called *khul'*. The Islamic method of divorce allows both spouses to think ahead before the final separation.

Misunderstandings about divorce have led Muslim men in some Muslim communities to frequently divorce wives or, on the

---

4. *Woman in Shari'ah* by Abdur Rahman I Doi, p92, Ta-Ha Publishers, London, 1989
5. *Role of Muslim Woman in Society* by Afzalur Rahman, p153, Sirah Foundation, London

contrary, refuse to grant divorce. Some of them keep their wives in suspense over their decision. All of these things are deplored in Islam. The Qur'an instructs men to '…let them go in an amicable manner…' (Qur'an 65:2).

It is important for Muslim society to realise that once marriage comes to a breaking point, amicable divorce is the only solution. Sadly, there is still some social stigma attached to the status of divorced women that needs to be removed. Divorced women have the same right to remarry as divorced men.

1.7 MARRIAGE AND FAMILIES

The natural fruit of marriage is the birth of children. Children are the products of physical love between a man and a woman. If the physical love occurs within the secure bounds of a loving marriage between a responsible man and woman, then this provides the best possible physical and emotional environment for the upbringing of a child.

When adolescent boys and girls think about marriage they intend to embark upon an irreversible life journey, and are destined never to be the same again. Before marriage individuals can apparently lead their life according to their own plans, although other adults might have influences over them. They adopt lifestyles and habits of their own or influenced by their parents or some other people. Their maturity and responsibility remain limited. But, once they tie the knot with another human being, their life changes altogether. Human love between the spouses shifts the centre of their world. They have the same parents, siblings, friends and colleagues, but the new person takes over many of their priorities in life. With two families coming closer, new relatives come into the picture. Many rights and responsibilities are opened up inadvertently and they feel obliged to take care of them. The newly-weds may initially find it hard to cope with all these demands, but gradually they settle down with time and experience and with the support of those around them.

The newly-weds need to spend some time exclusively with each other in order to understand each other's strengths and weaknesses. The concept of the 'honeymoon' probably derives from this urgency to give the couple some time and space. During this time, they may be at the height of their emotions and roam around in a world of idealism. However, after some time, they return to reality and need to re-assess their relationship in order to clarify their positions on some of the hard realities of life so that they can reorient the focus of their life and formulate their planning regarding livelihoods, broader family matters, social habits, having children, etc.

Couples who can adapt quickly to the new realities bring order and balance in their life. They find their life challenging but enjoyable. Some may lose balance altogether and tend to undermine their responsibilities to their own parents and others in the heat of the love for their spouse. Muslim life should always have balance and justice. Duties toward a spouse do not remove or override duties toward others in the family, to community and the *ummah*. All of them are important in their own place. A balanced person has the ability to work out priorities in rights and in responsibilities to Allah and His creatures.

However, the most important aspect of married life is the conscious choice to have children and to undertake their upbringing. Muslims never forget that the blessing of parenthood for a couple comes from Allah Who alone can create life. A right-acting couple will strive to bring up right-acting children and in their sincere efforts in this goal they rely on Allah alone. No human being has any control over whether or not a new life will come into a family as Allah says in the Qur'an:

> ...He bestows (children) male or female according to His Will (and Plan). Or He bestows both males and females, and He leaves barren whom He will... (Qur'an 42:49-50)

A couple should not be made to feel less in the eyes of society because they do not have children, or they do not have children of a certain gender, as this is all part of Allah's decree.

The conception, growth of the foetus in the womb and the birth of a child is a mystery and nobody knows whether a baby will be physically and mentally complete or born with some disability. It is truly a miracle of Allah to grant a couple a child and every child should be treated as a precious being. The Prophet Muhammad ﷺ advised Muslims to remember Allah in supplication at all times and even in the ecstatic moment of physical union.

In order to create the best possible environment for the upbringing of children, parenthood needs to start from the moment a man and woman start their married life, not after the child is actually born. Child-rearing is a considerable job in itself that involves creative planning, dedication and sacrifice. Looking after vulnerable young creatures, giving them warmth and love, providing them with comfort and security, and raising them in Islam, is more than a full-time commitment. A couple seeking the pleasure of Allah and looking for a meaningful life should be emotionally prepared to bear all these burdens. They sacrifice the comfort of life and happily accept the joyful pain of parenting.

Parenthood is a unique journey that brings challenges and rewards in married life. It can be the most pleasurable and worthwhile engagement in life. But parenting is more than just parenthood; it is a conscious and proactive endeavour to raise children in the way Allah wants. A couple's long-term plan is absolutely vital for the development of children's physical, intellectual, moral and spiritual life. Parenting becomes part of family life. Skills become necessary, particularly in complex post-modern societies.

'The hand that rocks the cradle rules the world'. Nations that cater for the proper nourishment and development of their children outperform others. Those who fail lose out.

1.8 EXECUTIVE SUMMARY

- Marriage between a man and a woman is the basis of family life; it legitimately fulfils the needs of the individual as well as society and is a *sunnah* of the Prophet ﷺ. Same-sex partnerships are detrimental to society and are *haram.*
- Young Muslims may choose their own partners or have assistance in doing so. Either way any contact between members of the opposite sex must be well within the bounds of Islam. Courting before marriage is *haram* but on the other hand it is advisable to try to get to know the person to some

extent before embarking on this major life journey. In any case, the consent of both the man and woman are essential.

- In choosing a marriage partner *taqwa* – awareness of Allah leading to avoiding acts of disobedience and embodiment of acts of obedience – should be given top priority, then there arises the need to look for areas of compatibility between them. Husbands and wives should recognise positive features in each other and overlook or forgive weaknesses.

- Early marriage is encouraged, especially in permissive societies. One should not wait for an 'ideal time' to start married life. However, a minimum level of economic solvency of the man and of the emotional and intellectual maturity of the couple are important.

- The marriage ceremony is a simple occasion in the presence of witnesses, with some prescribed requirements of *Shari'ah*. The marriage feast or *walima* should not be extravagant nor should there be unreasonable demands made by either party for material objects or money.

- Steadfastness and adherence to the commands of Allah are required to get through the difficult periods of marriage. If for genuine reasons a marriage fails, divorce is permissible in Islam, albeit disliked. When a husband divorces his wife it is called *talaq* and when a wife gets a divorce from her husband it is *khul'*.

- Children are a blessing from Allah and need to be looked after properly as gifts of Allah and raised in Islam so that they grow up to be responsible human beings. Steps should be taken at the start of marriage to create a wholesome Islamic environment for children to be brought up in. All children have the right to good parenting.

CHAPTER TWO

Family: An Islamic Perspective

O mankind! Be careful of your duty to your Lord Who has created you from a single self and from it created its mate and then disseminated many men and women from the two of them. Be careful of your duty toward Allah in Whose name you claim demands on one another, and toward the wombs (that bear you). Lo! Allah has been a Watcher over you.

(Qur'an 4:1)

2.1 THE FORTRESS FAMILY AND HUMAN CIVILISATION

The family has always been the bedrock of human society. It gives mooring, anchor, stability and tranquillity to its members. It provides affection and emotional support to infants and young children. It gives roots to older children. It teaches them values and responsibility in the wider social context.

The family is a primary social group united through bonds of kinship or marriage. It provides its members with protection, companionship and security. The family has evolved since the beginning of human history and the multiplicity of families has given rise to clans, tribes and races. It has been the cradle of human civilisation since Adam and Hawa, our first father and mother, who cultivated the earth and who, as husband and wife, formed the human race.

As the first human family proliferated into multitudes over the millennia, families have maintained their original nature, with a clear distinction between male and female roles; it being natural that when women gave birth and their duties looking after children grew onerous, the tasks outside the home of the men should grow more important. The physical and emotional features of men and women made this all the more natural. This has continued to be so in most societies until recent times. However, in modern technological countries, due to the needs of finance and industrial society, there are growing changes in the family structure and in the roles of men and women in society. As the number of children born to a woman decreases, her role in the family and society is also changing dramatically. The concept of a nuclear family with two adults and one or two children is becoming the norm, accompanied by an increase in single-parent families. With the rising demand for both men and women as workers in the financial-industrial complex and the trend for compensatory individualism and self-centredness, people are becoming cut off from a wider family network, giving rise to loneliness, depression and stress. The advent of modern technological gadgets has exacerbated these feelings, and people have little time for each other in the family.

Muslim families have been fortresses of Muslim civilisation and in them women play their creative and decisive roles in a way which is complementary to men. When the Mongol onslaught overpowered Muslim lands in the thirteenth century CE, many Muslim women were forcibly married to the conquering soldiers. Within a generation the victors became captives of Islam, due mainly to the exemplary qualities of the Muslim women.

Babies are born in a family fully dependent on the mercy of Allah whose most immediate agents are the parents. Their survival, physical and personal growth are linked to their family members. In all these aspects, the mother's role is vital. Throughout the history of Islam, Muslim mothers have been at the forefront of passing on the body and spirit of Islam to subsequent generations. Their self-esteem, confidence and pro-active and positive mothering have produced generations of creative and dynamic Muslims.

If a Muslim woman is in worship and remembrance of her Lord, she is a solace to her husband and a refuge for her children. If she is fulfilled in her worship of Allah, she is a source of happiness in the family, and the sweetness, joy, peace and tranquillity in the house depend largely on her. She is a reservoir of strength and confidence for her husband and children. Islamic history is full of stories of valiant mothers who guided and encouraged their sons in their struggle for justice. The Arabic saying, 'the mother is a school' places women in their proper perspective. In the same way if a man is a slave and worshipper of Allah and is engaged in working for the cause of Allah he is a source of strength to his wife and children.

During the decadent period, some of the *ummah* lost the vitality of Islam and degenerated, becoming sterile, with women experiencing some of the worst of it. As their situation worsened, the fortress of the Muslim family started crumbling. Consequently, Muslims everywhere are now struggling to recover from their intellectual stagnation and internal social haemorrhage. Unless Muslim family units, with women at the helm, are rejuvenated, the struggle to overcome Muslim impotence cannot be won.

Historically, while women were denied their rights elsewhere, it was Islam that gave them dignity. Islam has confirmed man and woman in complementary, not competitive, roles in the family and in society. Women are waived certain tasks, such as the burden of earning for the family so they can devote their time, energies and intellects to the sound raising of healthy, intelligent, committed Muslim children and the creation of a loving home environment. That does not preclude them from engaging in business or in any other suitable profession. In fact, Muslim communities everywhere desperately need educated and professional women. *Umm al-Mu'minin* Khadijah ﷠, the noble wife of the Prophet ﷺ, was a renowned business woman in her own right who, before Islam, appointed Muhammad ﷺ as her agent in trips to Syria.

The modern trend of 'the empowerment of women', invented mainly to bring women into the labour market, as well as the tremendous economic pressures arising from the usurious economy, are putting physical and psychological pressure on women, including Muslim mothers, to go out and earn and build 'careers' at the expense of their commitment to the family. Of course, women may need engagement with work and economic matters in their lives. The issue here needs to be properly understood. What sort of engagement and what is the priority in life? Considering the physical pressure and psychological stress in maintaining balance between the family and professional life many 'career women' in developed countries are now reducing their external commitments and returning to spend time with their children. They are learning the hard way that raising children is far more important than money and status, with the added benefit of also being very satisfying.

After all, maintaining a house and rearing children are complete and highly noble occupations in their own right. No one should be over-burdened in life.

> **Allah does not impose on any self any more than it can stand.** (Qur'an 2:286)

> **No burden bearer can bear another's burden.** (Qur'an 35:18)

Allah looks after the interests of both men and women. It is of course unfortunate that homemakers are still unrecognised, unappreciated and unremunerated in developed societies, in spite of the language of equality and rights.

2.2 MUSLIM FAMILIES: FEATURES AND PURPOSES

Muslim families have some unique features. They guard against the wanderings of the sexual appetites and channel them within the wholesome and meaningful pursuit of life. They help with the increase of human virtues, such as love, mercy, self-sacrifice and justice. They also provide a refuge from emotional and psychological disturbances of their members.[6] When families are centred on the worship and remembrance of Allah, they can be anchors of security and stability for human beings.

Muslim families have always been a source of inspiration for their members. In the earliest days of Islam, during the time of the Prophet ﷺ and in the following two generations, Muslim families played their most creative roles in the history of humankind. The admirable military generals, political strategists, intellectual leaders, scholars, traders – all sincere teachers of Islam – were the products of blessed Muslim families. In that, Muslim women played an outstanding role and left a long-lasting legacy that is appreciated to this day.

The family is the microcosm of a society and, as such, there are distinct roles for its members, as mentioned in the following hadith:

> Each one of you is a trustee (shepherd) and is accountable for that which is entrusted to him. A ruler is a trustee and is accountable for his trust, a man is a trustee in respect of his family, a woman is a trustee in respect of her husband's house and children. (Sahih al-Bukhari and Muslim)

---

6. *Women in Islam* by Aisha Lemu and Fatima Heeren, p38, The Islamic Foundation, UK, 1978

As the elementary unit of organised group life, a family has a leader, just as society must have a leader. The Creator of human beings has placed man in that leadership role within the family context and prescribed that women remain loyal to men, just as Allah prescribes that Muslim men are obedient and loyal to Muslim leaders. In the first two-member family, Adam was designated as the leader.

> **Men are in charge of women, because Allah has made the one of them to excel the other, and because they spend of their property (for the support of women). So good are the obedient, guarding in secret that which Allah has guarded.** (Qur'an 4:34).

> **... And they (women) have rights similar to those (of men) over them in kindness, and men are a degree above them. Allah is Mighty, Wise.** (Qur'an 2:228)

These *ayat* of the Qur'an on the issue of leadership in the family have been misunderstood by non-Muslims and even by many Muslims. Proponents of the radical feminist movement have attacked the 'inequality' of men and women in Islam with a view to undermining Muslim family structure.

Divine wisdom guides every Islamic ruling. A common-sense understanding based on human physiology and emotion will justify the fairness of the man-woman relationship in Islam. Over 1400 years ago Allah, exalted is He, eliminated the status of women as 'chattels', prohibited the pre-Islamic practice of female infanticide and gave women full control over their own earnings and wealth. Women are equal partners of men. They will be accountable to Allah on the Day of Judgement for their individual action. Allah has granted other rights to women, such as the right of inheritance, the right to initiate divorce and the right to earn or own a business. The wife of the Prophet Muhammad ﷺ, *Umm al-Mu'minin* Khadijah ﷺ, was the first person after the Prophet ﷺ to accept Islam. The first martyr, *shaheed*, in Islamic history was also a woman. The Qur'an has clarified that men and women are indispensable partners in human civilisation.

The believers, men and women, are protectors, one of another... (Qur'an 9:71)

The distribution of responsibility in a family setting is to make sure that human society is saved from chaos and disorder. In any human organisation individuals know their duties and their boundaries. To Allah, no human being is superior to another, except in *taqwa*.

Men and women who are Muslims, men and women who are muminun, men and women who are obedient, men and women who are truthful, men and women who are steadfast, men and women who are humble, men and women who give sadaqa, men and women who fast, men and women who guard their private parts, men and women who remember Allah much: Allah has prepared forgiveness for them and an immense reward. (Qur'an 33:35)

The noblest among you in Allah's sight is the one with the most taqwa. Allah is All-Knowing, All-Aware. (Qur'an 49:13)

Leadership in the family context means that a husband has the responsibility for making the major decisions concerning the family's loyalty to Islam and its well-being, after consultation with his wife. That includes decisions on all aspects of the implementation of the *deen*, responsibility for his family's upbringing and Islamic education as well as the worldly decisions on earning a *halal* income and maintaining the family. This latter is not only a moral but also a legal obligation. But he has no legal right over his wife's earnings, which are her own, unless she decides to spend for the family. Her priority is to look after her husband's property, their home and children, particularly with respect to a proper upbringing for the children in Islam. Conscientious husbands and wives work in consultation with each other in family affairs, but a wife is obliged to recognise her husband's right to lead the family, just as the husband may be consulted by his leader, *amir*, but must recognise and abide by the *amir's* decisions. Right-acting husbands and wives fear Allah and do not transgress the boundaries set by Him.[7]

> The Prophet ﷺ said: *The best woman is she who, when you see her you feel pleased, and when you direct her she obeys. She protects your rights and keeps her chastity when you are absent.* (Ibn Majah)

2.3 RIGHTS AND RESPONSIBILITIES IN THE FAMILY

Rights and responsibilities in human society are intertwined. One's responsibility is the other's right. The rights and responsibilities of husbands, wives, parents and children are inscribed in the *Shari'ah*. When they are fully complied with, families secure heavenly peace and make a positive impact on societies.

---

7. *Women in Islam* by Aisha Lemu and Fatima Heeren, p18, The Islamic Foundation, UK, 1978

In extended families, these rights and responsibilities stretch over generations of people connected together by blood or marriage. A general principle is that older people deserve respect, but have more responsibility.

Among parents

As husband and wife, parents in the family have rights over each other. Islam has asked a Muslim wife to observe the following:

- she should be thankful to Allah, a part of which is being grateful to her husband, as it is mentioned in a *hadith* that most of the women in the Fire are those who are ungrateful
- she should preserve her chastity
- when her husband wants her physical company she should not refuse
- she should look after the house and children effectively

And also without her husband's permission she should not:

- give charity from his property
- fast an optional fast
- leave the house
- invite into the house individuals, especially males, of whom he disapproves

On the other hand, from her husband a wife has the right to:

- love
- respect
- fair treatment
- dignified maintenance

In a Muslim family, husbands should be considerate and far from arrogant. For husbands, the Prophet Muhammad ﷺ should be their role model.

Between Parents and Children

It is incumbent on parents to provide their children with basic human necessities – such as food, clothing, shelter, love, affection, Islamic upbringing and to take care of their health. This is treated as an *'ibadah* for the parents. It is also important for parents to teach their children courtesy (*adab*), and to treat them with respect, and give them security, warmth and compassion. Above all, as human beings comprised of body and spirit, parents must provide their children with important life skills and spiritual nourishment. All these are rights of children in *Shari'ah*. Qur'an refers to a wise sage, Luqman, who exhorted his son on this (Qur'an 31:13-19).

The following *hadith* also speak of parental responsibility to the children:

> *A father can give his child nothing better than good manners.* (At-Tirmidhi)

> *Be careful to your duty to Allah and be fair and just to your children.* (Sahih al-Bukhari)

> *Whoever properly brings up two daughters until they reach maturity, that man and myself (the Prophet ﷺ) will be as close in Paradise as two adjacent fingers.* (Sahih Muslim)

On the other hand, children have their share of responsibilities to their parents. They can never repay their debts to their parents. However, they should try to reciprocate by helping them out in times of necessity, especially in their frailty. They should help parents in household chores and in any other work asked by them. They must not use such language or show attitudes towards parents that hurt them. Their gratitude to their parents, especially to their mothers who bore so much pain for them, is a divine requirement (Qur'an 2:83, 4:36, 17:23-24, 29:8, 31:14, 46:15).

There are many *hadith* regarding children's responsibilities toward their parents. The following are some of them:

> *Allah's Messenger* ﷺ *said thrice, "Shall I not inform you of the biggest of the great wrong actions?" We said, "Yes, Messenger of Allah." He said, "To join partners in worship of Allah, to be ungrateful to one's parents…"* (Sahih al-Bukhari)

> *A man came to the Messenger of Allah* ﷺ *and asked permission to go on jihad. The Prophet* ﷺ *asked him, "Are your parents alive?" The man said, "Yes." The Prophet* ﷺ *responded, "Then strive to serve them."* (Sahih al-Bukhari and Muslim)

> *A man came to the Prophet* ﷺ *and asked, "Who among people is most entitled to kind treatment from me?" He answered, "Your mother." The man asked, "Then who?" He said, "Your mother." "Then who?", the man asked. The Prophet* ﷺ *said, "Your mother." The man asked, "Then who?" The Prophet* ﷺ *said, "Then your father."* (Sahih al-Bukhari and Muslim)

> *Paradise lies at the feet of your mother.* (An-Nasa'i)

> *A father's pleasure is Allah's pleasure, a father's displeasure is Allah's displeasure.* (At-Tirmidhi)

Among Children

Children are the flowers in a family garden. Although they carry the same parental 'blood' in them and share many similar characteristics, all of them are different and unique. As flowers in a garden with a variety of colours and fragrances increase its beauty, children with various physical and mental characteristics make the family elegant. Some children in the family become vocal, loud, vibrant and impulsive, while others become reflective, mature and quiet. These unique features of individuals make families with children blessed. Of course, many of the personality traits grow and take shape due to situational influence.

Whatever the differences within individuals in a family, parents and all the children enjoy and learn from one another. Children have their mutual rights and responsibilities. Obviously, from an Islamic point of view, elders have more responsibilities than the youngsters in a family. The elder brothers or sisters have a special place of respect in relation to the younger ones as well. In terms of respect they are next to parents. They often help the younger brothers and sisters grow through their experiences of life and the younger ones generally look to them as role models. They help their younger siblings in education and transmitting life skills to them. They sometimes take them to school, parks and other places of interest. They play with them and give them invaluable joy in life. In any case, they become the effective educators or mentors of their brothers and sisters. Elder brothers and sisters can work to bridge any communication difficulties between parents and younger siblings.

The younger ones are asked to listen to their elders and respect them. This love and respect is a result of the kindness that the younger ones receive from their elders; it cannot be forcibly demanded. Sibling arguments, complaints or even fights are the signs of liveliness in the family, unless they create nuisance or danger. In most cases, the elders should be able to handle them with maturity and authority. Together all members of a family have a collective role, to grow together as Muslims, maintain the dignity of the family and contribute to the common good of humanity.

2.4 IMPORTANT ISSUES CONCERNING THE FAMILY

The Spirit of the Extended Family

Families, clans and tribes have been the sources of prestige and socio-political and economic status in the past and this is true even today in many societies. Extended families, in which three or more generations live under the same family umbrella, help Muslims to acquire many social qualities, such as self-sacrifice, compromise for the sake of the common good, mutual respect, affection and mutual consultation. Human beings are always interdependent. The nature of their dependence on others as babies or as frail elders may be different, but is in principle the same.

> **When We grant long life to people, We return them to their primal state (back to weakness after strength). So will you not use your intellect?** (Qur'an 36:67)

Old age is a feared reality of life. Imam Abu Hanifa, an intellectual giant in early Islam, was once heard to make a thoughtful remark on this that meant (sic) – 'when you first see grey hairs in your head welcome the new phase of your life'. It can be a painful stage of life where human beings, after passing through an era of physical strength and mental agility, may lose their grip on themselves and their surroundings. The supplication of Khalif Umar ﷺ for the death of a martyr for himself before the frailty of old age reflected his wisdom. After a life of strength it is painful to be dependent on others even if it is on the children who were once reared with immense love and pain. In modern societies where individualism is threatening family life, older people can feel sidelined and unimportant, even ending up in care or at the mercy of social services.

Old age is a golden age. It is the phase of wisdom and collected experience in one's life and as such can be of enormous help to the extended family. Being surrounded by young people keeps one connected to the future, while the company of elders helps to remind one of one's roots and heritage. It is common humanity and an important responsibility that older people are looked after by the younger generation. If, for some reason, families fail, society should of course become the safety net. It is cruel and inhuman that young and capable children enjoy their life, while their parents carry the burden of old age alone or in care. Children, who would definitely have perished without the support and love from their parents in their own childhood, have the responsibility to do the same for their parents when they need it most.

The virtue in the extended family arises from this humane attitude towards life. An extended family is like a miniature society where the wisdom of the elders, vitality of the youth and liveliness of the children keep buzzing and create a sense of togetherness among the members. There may be some natural difficulties and hardship in this arrangement, such as lack of privacy and individual space, but with good planning and considerate leadership they can be minimised and the benefits reaped. Moreover, experiencing some sacrifice is important for success in life.

An extended family is not necessarily one in which all its members live under the same roof. The whole philosophy of the extended family system is to share with, care for and support each other. If properly managed, children from extended families learn better and are better equipped with vital social and life skills than others. The grandparents are also excellent educators and 'child-minders' in times of necessity. Extended families in Muslim societies have produced superior results compared to the 'nuclear family' structure of modern industrialised societies.

> **Goodness in the extended family** – The experience of a family close to me has given me insight into the blessing of an extended family. They are a huge family, consisting of grandparents, married sons and daughters with their own children (grandchildren) and some yet unmarried children living as extended family members. They do not live under one roof, but all the sons and daughters live close by and under one leadership, the grandfather. In his late sixties he still has a full grip on family affairs. Every adult is busy with a job, study or business. He guides them, helps them when needed and decides, with consultation, on important aspects of the family. The sons and daughters listen to him, respect him and give him full support. The most prominent feature in the family is everybody's healthy interaction, not only among themselves, but with anyone who mixes with them. If people visit any of them, they immediately realise that they are the guests of everyone in the family. Even the young children, who are

normally busy in their own world of play, come, greet them and talk to them with warmth. "This is amazing," said one of his friends who has been struggling to imbue some social qualities in his own children.

He is getting older and weaker. So, on one occasion I asked him, "What do you think is going to happen when you cannot lead any more?"

He was not so sure. "There will be natural separation, but I believe they will cling together, insha'Allah. The necessity of staying together is far more important in permissive societies than in Muslim societies," he commented.

I was amazed at his insight. If all Muslims could follow elders like him in this regard, a lot of our fears and problems may be solved in the cushion of this supportive and loving network.

Domestic Violence

In modern societies, many young people are now becoming parents without acquiring the necessary sense of responsibility and accountability in life, nor having the required family or social structure needed for support. The emphasis is now on the individual, to gratify their passing desires and 'enjoy' themselves, often in the pursuit of material things. This is making it harder for families to live together in harmony.

Unfortunately, this trend is also being reflected within the Muslim community. Family helplines run by Muslims in recent years have recorded that verbal and physical abuse within Muslim families is on the rise. The causes of the violence are linked to alcohol, drug and substance abuse, extra-marital affairs, unemployment-related frustration, media influence, financial pressures, interference of the in-laws, etc. Many Muslim men treat their wives very strictly in the name of Islam. Their understanding of women's right is very shallow and they only adopt rigidity in dealing with their womenfolk, believing that women were created to serve men and their families at home and in the kitchen. These ideas have no place in Islam and stem from sheer ignorance. The role of a wife is not that of an unpaid servant of the household.

As well as the woman suffering, the result of any abuse is distressing to children who are caught in the crossfire of this family squabble, and who become pawns in the family disintegration. This may lead to problems at school and in forming relationships in later life and thus the cycle of violence may be perpetuated.

If all members of the family have a true understanding of their respective roles and responsibilities and adhere to the commands of Allah, then much tension and family difficulty can be avoided. The Prophet Muhammad ﷺ said:

> The best of the Muslims is he from whose hand and tongue the Muslims are safe. (Muslim)

> The best of you are those who are best to their families, and I am the best of you to my family. (At-Tirmidhi)

Fostering and 'Adoption' in Islam

Fostering is the act of taking care of another's child when that child's parents are dead or unable to look after the child themselves, for any reason.

Adoption, in the legal sense in which it is used in many Western countries, is not allowed in Islam. In the Western sense of adoption, the adopted child becomes the child of the adoptive parents and takes on their family name.

In Islam, fostering or adoption does not make children, sons or daughters in all respects. For example, the laws of inheritance do not apply to them in the same way that it does to biological children. The fostered children must maintain their biological father's name, so that there is no doubt as to the paternity of the child. However, they are to be loved, cared, raised and provided for in the same way as one's biological children. They should enjoy the privileges that the natural children do. The Qur'an has given clear guidelines on this:

> **... nor has He (Allah) made your adopted sons your actual sons. These are just words by your mouths. But Allah speaks the truth and He guides to the Way. Call them after their fathers. That is closer to justice in Allah's sight. But if you do not know their fathers' name, then they are your brothers in faith and people under your patronage.** (Qur'an 33:4-5)

There are many reasons why a Muslim couple may choose to foster a child. It may be that the couple has not been blessed with children of their own and fostering allows them the chance to raise children and fulfil their parental desires.

The practice of fostering orphan children is also highly desirable in Islam. The rights of orphans are mentioned numerous times in the Qur'an (Qur'an 2:220, 4:2, 4:6, 4:10, 4:127, 17:34). Indeed the Prophet Muhammad ﷺ raised a freed slave, Zayd bin Harith,

in his home like his son and he spoke of the virtues of taking care
of an orphan:

> *"I and the person who looks after an orphan will be in Paradise
> together like this..." - then he raised his forefinger and middle finger
> together.* (Sahih al-Bukhari)

There are a number of Muslim orphans in non-Muslims countries
that are in care or have been placed in non-Muslim homes.
Muslims in these countries should feel a sense of responsibility to
ensure that these innocent Muslim orphans are being brought up
within a wholesome Muslim environment and do whatever they
feel is within their means to address this problem.

2.5 MODERN THREATS TO THE FAMILY

Families in developed countries are now facing challenges from
many quarters. With increased pressure to survive and succeed,
human beings are unfortunately compromising with their inner
selves and with the higher values of life. Since the industrial
revolution women have been required to take part in economic
activities. As the balance in the gender role has tilted, it has forced
a turning point in family and social dynamics. During the Second
World War, as millions of young men fought and died, more
women were thrown into the world of work. The proponents of
materialistic ideas took this further and started defining women's
role as 'competitive' rather than 'complementary' and in terms
of unqualified 'equality' rather than 'equity'. The imbalance in
gender roles thus has a negative influence on the attitude toward
marriage, family and conception.

The traditional marriage-based family has been threatened with a number of alternatives in the modern societies, namely cohabitation, single-parenthood and homosexuality. It is important for Muslims to be aware of these pitfalls and take care not to fall into these.

a) Cohabitation

As the institution of marriage is facing more challenges, it is gradually being replaced by cohabitation, a situation where a couple live with each other without being legally married. Not so long ago, cohabitation was thought of as 'living in sin'. More recently, it was a temporary phenomenon, leading eventually to marriage. But, increasingly it has been observed that couples are now spending more time in cohabitation and may not even marry in the end. Why many people are leaving aside marriage as a social norm and adopting cohabitation is a complex question. Obviously, there are historical, moral, social and economic factors. The weakening of religious or spiritual values in people, fear of the burden of a long-term commitment to marriage, unwillingness to compromise and sacrifice for another person, the growing opportunities for women to develop lives for themselves outside marriage, the removal of the stigma of 'unmarried mothers' and 'illegitimate children' with the social acceptance of cohabitation and the recognition of children born out of wedlock are some of the main factors for this increase.

b) Single parenthood

Single parenthood may arise due to the death of one spouse, divorce, separation, desertion by one partner or result from a deliberate choice. There may be economic and other factors involved that lead people to choose to remain single parents. Whatever the reasons, the vast majority of single parents are women. The rise in single-parenthood is linked with the increase in the divorce rate and also to an increase in births outside marriage. As society is adjusting to this 'emerging form' of the family, it is gradually being treated as the norm.

Often in modern societies, the single parent has no support system from other family members and lives in isolation, having to do the job of two parents. This has a high social and economic cost. With only one parent around, children grow under the care of half parenting. The vital component of the other half is missing. This has an emotional effect as well. In most cases, one parent cannot cope with earning a livelihood and looking after the whole well-being of a child or children at the same time. This puts single parents at a perpetual disadvantage in society and it is no coincidence that single parenthood is sometimes associated with low living standards.

While single parent families will always exist in Muslim communities, due to death and divorce, the key difference should be that the Muslim single parent and their child(ren) should always have the support of family members and, if that is not available, then the support of the other Muslim members of the community. This will ensure that the parent is well able to cope with the pressures and demands of an already difficult situation and that the children do not feel their loss so keenly. This is where the spirit of the extended family and of the Muslim community is especially useful, indeed necessary.

c) Homosexuality

In recent decades, gay rights lobbies have been wielding much influence in the social and political arena of many developed societies. As a result, homosexuality is gradually becoming an accepted social norm in many countries.

Past nations, such as the nation of Lut ﷺ incurred the wrath of Allah when they accepted such practices. Yet the same situation presents itself again. Like the two other Abrahamic faiths, Islam is unequivocal in maintaining that a sexual relationship can only be between a man and woman in marriage. Recently, the British House of Lords ruled that "a homosexual couple in a stable relationship can be defined as a family". 'Same-sex marriage' or civil partnership is now legally accepted in many countries. Giving these partnerships the same legal status as marriage may be the social trend in some societies, but it is not acceptable in any transcendental religion.

Before this issue divides our community as it has done others before, Muslims should be united in arguing the case against homosexuality, albeit in a civilised manner. Islam does not promote violence or incite hatred against any people because of their lifestyle, but Muslims have a duty to argue for what they believe with patience and wisdom (Qur'an 41:34).

2.6 PROSELYTISATION AND THE CHALLENGE

It cannot be denied that throughout history women have suffered, as indeed have men. This has been as a result of deviation from divine truth, using religion as a cover to oppress women and women's lack of sustained confidence in standing up to injustices in the past. However, over the millennia many champions of human rights, prophets and other sages, have fought for gender equity within the institution of the family and social context. The advent of Islam 1400 years ago ushered in a new era with a dignified position for women in the world. Families, on the basis of justice and respect for both men and women, have proved to be the sources of Muslim glory. Muslim families became the centres of the mundane and spiritual meaning of life, and a life-long school. Muslim children were moulded by the universal nature of Islam, as they grew with confidence in the value-rich family environment. This contributed to the emergence of a Muslim civilisation with its dazzling contribution to human life. But, unfortunately, due to the political and intellectual sterility of most parts of the Muslim world in the last few centuries, human beings have virtually lost a balanced view of life in all these matters.

In the post-modern moral maze, all values related to human life, for example, marriage, family, sex, etc., are now losing their ethical and spiritual dimensions. It is a frightening scenario for all of us alive today and the situation does not seem to be improving for the foreseeable future.

It is encouraging that in recent times there has been a growing sense of urgency in bringing back the moral and ethical dimensions in the debate on marriage and family. Many high-flying career men and women, from corporate business to politics, are now reassessing their priorities and realising that providing for a family is more than career and prosperity, and that life on earth is too precious to be measured in terms of status and wealth. Children and family are now once again being pushed to the fore of the social agenda. This realisation is bringing people from various communities and faith groups together and needs to be given further momentum. Muslim communities in modern societies should come forward pro-actively to forge alliances with pro-family groups in order to save this institution from further erosion. Family building with good Islamic values should be the priority now in order to ensure a future generation that is strong enough to withstand the onslaught of materialism.

2.7 EXECUTIVE SUMMARY

- The family is the bedrock of human civilisation, in which men and women have complementary roles. Man is the leader in the context of the family, but has rights and responsibilities. Children have the right to physical, intellectual and spiritual nourishment. Working for children's Islamic development is not less important than giving them food and good education.

- Muslim families are open families and often extended, unlike contemporary closed, nuclear families of modern societies. A Muslim home provides a base for its members where right action is promoted and wrong action is minimised. The family is a centre of love and mercy. However, love for Allah and His Prophet ﷺ supersedes everything.

- Muslim families should have certain features to make them sources of inspiration for their members and others in the community. Through consultation and active participation of all family members, Muslims perform their divine and social responsibilities in this primordial human organisation.

- Fostered children or step-children should be treated in the same way as the couple's own children. No child in the family should have any restrictions placed on his or her growth.

- Parents must know what happens in the wider society in order to raise their children with positive Islamic values and with the ethos of social inclusiveness. Openness and clarity are essential for creating a learning environment in the family. Family loyalty is vital to the members. Sacrifice from the parents enhances the family bond and creates an Islamic ethos for children.
- Muslim families should make sure they are not 'ghettoised'. Muslims have obligations to their neighbours and to the wider society. Muslim children should be raised with a positive Muslim identity so that they are confident in interacting and engaging with other human beings.

CHAPTER THREE

Blessed Family and Nation Building

Our Lord, give us joy
in our spouses and children
and make us a good example
for those who have taqwa.

(Qur'an 25:74)

3.1 INGREDIENTS OF A BLESSED FAMILY

The family, being the bedrock of human society, is a noble institution and as such it universally needs to be preserved. It should not only be defended robustly, but should be promoted with passion and conviction. The promotion or rejection of family values is linked to the perception of life on earth and the role of man and woman in human history. Those who have a firm belief in divine revelation cannot conceive of weakening the family structure.

The foundation of a relationship between a man and a woman needs to be based on solid values such as long-term commitment, responsibility and maturity. It is then upon this solid foundation that families can stand firm and weather the storms that life brings. Infatuation, romance and 'a good time' in themselves are not strong enough bases on which to build a family. Marriage and families connect people to each other and anchor them in a life-long commitment. It is hard for short-sighted and selfish people to look beyond immediate pleasure, and so they engage themselves in fulfilling their desire for mere physical satisfaction. Even if they do form families they are rarely successful since the solid foundation is missing. An unhappy family creates disaffection, pain and frustration that give rise to crushed personalities full of confusion for all concerned. A healthy, balanced family life gives rise to healthy and balanced individuals and the reverse is also true. Frustrated young people raised in unhappy families may sooner or later vent that frustration and anger against society and thus society suffers the consequences. Dysfunctional families rob children of their happiness.

On the contrary, a happy family is the reservoir of positive parenting. It brings a sense of belonging, anchor and roots that build balanced personalities within children, who then contribute positively to society. Children growing up in blessed families are equipped with the tools to create blessed societies. The following are the major ingredients of blessed families, but the list is by no means exhaustive.

The Ingredients

Love

Love is at the core of family life. It can achieve things that cannot be achieved by force. Love captivates, influences, and moves things to happen. It penetrates deep into the self. It is the gel that produces a rock-solid relationship among people. Love is imbedded in human nature and a gift from Allah. Human history has exceptional stories of love. Love is power and as such has the capacity to build or burn human societies. Love emanates from the core of the heart. Hearts join and create fountains of love between two people, the father and mother. The arrival of a child in the family makes this love intense. As such, 'Father And Mother, I Love You' is an excellent acronym of FAMILY.

Love for one's own children is natural, as they are a blessed product of physical love between a man and a woman. Obviously, love between a husband and wife, two adults people with two distinct personalities, needs careful nurturing from both. Pure physical attraction cannot create love or maintain it for long, although that is not to say that it is not an important ingredient in marriage. People looking for family life over physical attraction have the rewards of permanent love on their side and the best chance of success. The Islamic vision of life in the family makes love exceptionally rewarding. In any situation, the 'joining' of hearts is due to Allah's special blessing. Wealth and beauty are not to be despised, but they cannot buy love.

> **And (as for the believers) Allah has unified their hearts. If you had spent everything on the earth you could not have unified their hearts, but Allah has unified them. He is Almighty, All Wise.** (Qur'an 8:63).

> **Some people set up equals to Allah, loving them as they should love Allah. But those who have iman have greater love for Allah.** (Qur'an 2:165)

> **Say: 'If your fathers or your sons or your brothers or your wives or your tribe, or any wealth you have acquired, or any business you fear may slump, or any house which pleases you, are dearer to you than Allah and His Messenger and doing jihad in His Way, then wait until Allah brings about His command. Allah does not guide people who are deviators.'** (Qur'an 9:24)

Love between parents is a reservoir where children find their sanctuary, if that love results from a higher love of Allah and His Messenger ﷺ. Parental love transmits naturally to children. Lack of even the basic level of love between parents may be the cause of emotional disturbance in children. Mechanical or loveless parenting results in children that lack the necessary emotional skills to cope with the emptiness in their lives.

Love has external manifestations and that is a natural part of the expression of love. However, the love between a husband and wife should not be so ostentatious that it becomes indecent and provocative in the public eye.

Mercy

Mercy is at the heart of family and social life. Allah, "Most Gracious, Most Merciful" (Qur'an 1:2), has created man out of His mercy and demands from us the same. The Qur'an has also used the word *rahmah* (mercy) to describe the relationship among Muslims.

> **Muhammad is the Messenger of Allah; and those who are with him are strong against unbelievers, (but) full of mercy among themselves.** (Qur'an 48:29)

In a Muslim family, because of the actual relationship and the presence of Islam, the manifestation of mercy among its members is more pronounced. The Prophet Muhammad ﷺ was the symbol of mercy to his family, his companions, the *ummah* of Muslims, mankind at large and the universe.

> **We have only sent you as a mercy to all the worlds.** (Qur'an 21:107)

Mercy is an important quality to be nurtured as the following *hadith* show:

> *Have mercy on those in the land, so that the One in Heaven will have mercy on you.* (Sunan al-Tirmidhi)

Allah is kind and He loves kindness in all affairs. (Sahih al-Bukhari and Muslim)

He who is deprived of leniency is deprived of goodness. (Sahih Muslim)

When Allah, the Exalted, wills some good towards the people of a household, He introduces kindness among them. (Musnad, Sahih al-Ja'mi)

Allah loves kindness and rewards it in such away that He does not reward for harshness or anything else. (Sahih Muslim)

Respect and Honour

He is not of us who has no compassion for our little ones and does not honour our old ones. (At-Tirmidhi)

Human beings are the manifestation of the divine will, and Allah has breathed spirit into each of them. Each one of us ought to show due respect to the other. Every human being has the potential of doing something, although some are obviously more capable than others. The test in this world is to see who can maximise their efforts to the best of their ability and for the pleasure of Allah. The act of respect is the recognition of that worth. Respect is reciprocal – if someone is given respect, there is every likelihood that the other will reciprocate that. Allah expects Muslims to show respect to others.

Each child grows with certain personality traits. Every individual should therefore be respected for their unique combination of traits. Respect for an individual is thus natural and brings happiness.

We can all learn from each other, even from tiny babies. Everyone has views on different aspects of life. Respect for each other's knowledge and freedom of expression give rise to fellow feeling, motivation and creativity. The formulation and expression of knowledge depend on family and social environment.

Even though family members may live under the same roof, each person has a world of their own that needs to be respected. As children grow older, they need to learn the etiquette of a Muslim house. Islam teaches decency, and family is the first institution where they should learn it. For example, Islam requires members of the household to seek permission when entering each other's rooms. Parents, of course, need to know what is happening in their children's worlds and should endeavour to implement a positive ethos with full honesty and without being intrusive and insensitive. Like everyone else, children need their own space and time. Conscientious parents allow space for their children to grow and develop with self-respect and respect for others, especially for older people including elder brothers and sisters.

Members of a family are expected to maintain the honour of the family by their positive behaviour and defending it from external threat. Islam considers it a disgrace if people undermine their own family and community. However, that honour should be based on Islamic spirit, not other factors such as tribalism.

Loyalty

Loyalty has a relational aspect and a wider meaning. The minimum requirement in a family is that husband and wife must be loyal to each other in their marital relationship. Infidelity in marriage is a grave wrong action, punishable in the harshest manner. While fidelity is rewarding in both worlds, infidelity brings suspicion, mental torture, frustration and a 'hellish' atmosphere in this world and a real Hell in the Hereafter unless Allah turns to one in forgiveness. Loyalty to each other in the family is enhanced by love and respect.

A family is bonded by marriage and blood ties and is one of the keys to group life. Family loyalty thus gives a part of the identity of a member of the family.

However, without proper understanding this can create a narrow sense of pride and produce 'family feuds' as is often seen in many societies. A family blends together through loyalty and trust among its members to create a wider unit. In the history of humankind, family loyalty grew into tribal loyalty and created kingdoms and civilisations on the one hand and destroyed them on the other. *'Asabiya* (or familial and tribal loyalty) was at the heart of pre-Islamic Arab character. Islam refined its dynamic and powerful features with a view to creating a community, the *ummah*. Its potent force held sway and created an unparalleled dynamism in the history of mankind, as uniquely explained by Ibn Khaldun.

Patience and Forgiveness

People living close together, sharing space and other material resources, need understanding, compromise and sacrifice. Human beings have both 'evil and good' traits in their character (Qur'an 91:8) and as such have innate strengths and weaknesses. Close people, parents and children, living under the same roof definitely experience this in each other. Intelligent are those who acknowledge, understand and overlook weaknesses and live with them, unless they are serious. Of course, we all need to improve ourselves and try sensitively to encourage others to improve also. But negative features of family members and others should not occupy our minds. Those who can see things positively live in peace and harmony. Cynics often suffer and intolerant people lose out. They are the source of dissension in society. The reasons for family breakdown in many cases are due to the lack of compromise on smaller issues. Insensitive and sometimes silly comments and counter comments raise tension between family members leading to arguments and shouting matches. A wonderful piece of advice from the Qur'an can put things into perspective.

> **Live together with them correctly and courteously. If you dislike them, it may well be that you dislike something in which Allah has placed a lot of good.**
> (Qur'an 4:19)

A family or a society remains divided and can even break up in recrimination if patience and forgiveness wear thin among its members. These are the qualities of big hearts that bring immense reward from Allah (see Qur'an 3:159, 7:199, 42:43). Patience is a great quality that needs to be sought from Allah (see Qur'an 2:153).

Sacrifice

> **But (they) give preference over themselves, even though they themselves are needy. And who so is saved from his own avarice – such are they who are successful.**
> (Qur'an 59:9)

> **You will not attain piety until you expend of what you love; and whatever thing you expend, God knows of it.**
> (Qur'an 3:92)

Sacrifice has many dimensions. Spending of time, energy and wealth in the Way of Allah is the highest mission in life for a Muslim. It emanates from a conscious understanding of what it means. Sacrifice is an inescapable ingredient in the world of creating an Islamic civilisation. It is linked to self-surrender to Allah and the fullest conviction in Islam. It is an essential building block that builds individuals' characters in order that they may play meaningful roles on earth. The sacrifice of the earlier generations of Islam, in the wake of apparently insurmountable barriers, was the stepping stone for the ascendancy of Islam. The history of humankind teaches one single message: sacrifice is at the core of victory.

The primary sacrifice in a family begins when a mother sacrifices her comforts during pregnancy. Nine months of carrying a growing foetus in the womb, being ever watchful that it is properly nourished inside and saved from harm, prepares her for more sacrifice when the baby is born. Her eating habits, sleep, rest, work – are all programmed to revolve around the tiny creature. Throughout infancy, both father and mother willingly reorganise their lives, day after day, to adjust themselves to the needs of the little baby. As the child grows, the necessity for sacrifice takes different forms. Every time a new baby arrives in the house their sacrifices multiply. Unfortunately, the fear of this sacrifice has lead some people to avoid children altogether or limit their number for selfish reasons.

Earning for the family and spending on its members cannot happen without the spirit of sacrifice. Parents often sacrifice their careers, work harder and earn more money only to bring comfort to their children, pay for a good education and attempt to guarantee successful lives for them. It is short-sighted to think that it is a burden for children or other family members to share in the earnings of the breadwinner, but this is a small sacrifice for a much larger reward that cannot be purchased at any price.

Sacrificing one's opinions and ego is also important for the success of family life. It is essential to achieve greater harmony in the community and this is the area in which many people fail. Muslims, of course, have strong views on the basic tenets of Islam, where there is no room for compromise. But those basic issues are only a few. Islam demands sacrifice for the wider benefit of human beings, their family, society, the *ummah* and, in fact, the whole of humanity.

Justice and Fairness

O you who believe, be steadfast witnesses for Allah in equity and let not the hatred of any people incite you to depart from justice. Be just, that is closer to piety... (Qur'an 5:8)

Allah commands justice and doing good and giving to relatives,... (Qur'an 16:90)

Justice is at the heart of Allah's creative design. The creation of the Garden and the Fire is to bring about final justice, as the earthly life is too short to establish justice. The Arabic words, *qist* and *'adl* are very wide indeed. They are intertwined with the implementation of Truth. The manifest balance and proportion in the creation is the reflection of Allah's justice in the universe. Maintaining a proper balance between rights and responsibilities is the essence of justice.

Justice in the family does not necessarily mean equal shares in everything for everyone. In the real world, justice means equitable and balanced dealings. Most importantly, dealing in the family should not be seen as unjust and unfair, especially by the children. We may not be fully aware, but children are keen observers of what happens around them and what their parents say or do. It is important that parents attain an extra degree of consciousness in their behaviour and dealings. The family is a mini-community and justice established there has an impact on the wider society.

Tiny things, little words and small actions matter to children. It is difficult to believe that Muslim parents would be unfair or unjust to one or the other child. But every child is different. One child may be more intelligent, more observant of religion, always willing to listen or has some other qualities over the others. Moreover, a parent may prefer a boy or a girl for some emotional reasons. All these can invite the special attention of a parent towards a particular child. The Prophet Ya'qub صلى had a special liking for his beloved son Yusuf صلى over others for genuine reasons. What it means is that, even if parents are emotionally warmer towards one child, they should not visibly discriminate against others, as this will cause loss of confidence in the child.

Consultation

Allah has commanded believers to conduct their affairs and settle their differences in consultation.

> ... **So pardon them, and ask forgiveness for them and consult with them upon the conduct of affairs. And when you have reached a firm decision, put your trust in Allah. Allah loves those who put their trust in Him.**
> (Qur'an 3:159)

...and those who manage their affairs by mutual consultation... (Qur'an 42:38)

Consultation is in the spirit of social life, and the Prophet Muhammad ﷺ practised it in his domestic and public life. In order to teach his *ummah* the importance of consultation he even decided to go against his own ideas in some cases, for example before the Battle of Uhud. During the Treaty of Hudaybiya when the Muslims failed to comprehend the impending victory and were reluctant to follow his verbal instruction regarding the 'Umra (lesser pilgrimage) he consulted Umm Salama ﵂, his wife who was accompanying him, as to what to do. Her unique suggestion came as a blessing from Allah and healed all. (This episode also emphasises the importance of a husband consulting with his wife.)

Although the final decision is made by the head of the family, consultation produces confidence, trust, interest, mutual respect and team spirit within its members. It shows individual members of the family that their opinions are valued and it enhances their sense of responsibility and input. All of these things are essential for any venture to succeed. However, consultation needs diligence and relevance and should not go around in a circle. Proper decision making is important. If misconstrued, it could lead to indecision or no decision. Spirited consultation helps cure the diseases of arrogance and egotism. It is the pillar of a successful social life. In Islam consultation is the life-blood of social health.

Consultation in a family is essential for creating a positive and lively environment. It builds a bond between husband and wife. It helps them plan for the family, household chores and effective parenting. As children grow they should be involved in the process of consultation, particularly in affairs that affect them. It helps the whole family to sail through difficulties in modern life, as 'two brains are always better than one'. There is immense blessing in consultation.

Honesty and Integrity

Surely truth leads to virtue and virtue leads to the Garden. (Sahih al-Bukhari)

Guarantee me six things and I shall assure you of the Garden – When you speak, speak the truth; keep your promise; discharge your trust; guard your chastity: lower your gaze; and withhold your hands from highhandedness. (Al-Bayhaqi)

Honesty, integrity and trustworthiness are the essence of a Muslim. These are also basic leadership qualities. In a family context the father is the leader. Sons and daughters emulate their fathers and mothers as role models in different ways. Muslim parents thus need to be honest, not only because it makes them better parents but because they are accountable to Allah for their actions.

Parents are like shepherds at home. Honest and truthful parents create exemplary qualities in their children through words and deeds. The following story tells us how Muslim mothers trained the teachers of humanity.

Honesty has its fruit – Abd al-Qadir al-Jaylani is known as a great saint and teacher of Islam. He is also noted for his knowledge and wisdom. His father died when he was very young, so his righteous mother brought him up. Through

Allah's mercy and by her efforts he grew up with a thirst for knowledge. As he was finishing his education in a local school the young Abd al-Qadir learnt that Baghdad was famous for its scholars and people of knowledge. With his mother's permission he decided to go there. When the time came he prepared for the journey and joined a caravan that was going to Baghdad. His mother gave him forty gold Dinars so that he could live independently in Baghdad and concentrate fully on education. As a precaution she sewed them into the lining of his clothes so that no one could see them or hear their noise. She also told him that whatever might happen to him he should never tell a lie, even if telling the truth would cost him his life.

On the way bandits attacked the caravan and all the people were robbed of their possessions. One of the bandits asked young Abd al-Qadir whether he had anything valuable with him. Abd al-Qadir, without hesitation said, "Yes, I have forty gold Dinars." They would not believe him in the beginning, but the innocent face of the boy said he was not telling a lie. "Where are they?" asked the leader. "They are sewn into my clothes," replied Abd al-Qadir. They tore the lining of the clothes open and could see the shining Dinars. The bandit leader was overwhelmed by the truthfulness of the boy and asked, "Why did you tell us about the money?" "My mother advised me never to tell a lie, even if speaking the truth would cost my life. How could I disregard her?" replied the boy without any fear or sense of loss.

The leader was taken aback, thought for a while and looked at his gang. Everybody was speechless. A feeling of remorse attacked him from inside. How could he rob people when he knew perfectly well that what he was doing was completely wrong? His instinct was telling him to repent, and he did so immediately asking his men to return everything they had stolen.[8]

Openness and Clarity

The implementation of Islam created societies where openness and transparency, on one hand, and accountability, on the other, worked hand in hand. Muslims abhor suspicion and spying on each other, in the family and in society. They are not only unethical but criminal acts as well. They eat away the trust among people.

> **O you who believe, avoid most suspicion. Indeed some suspicion is a crime. And do not spy and do not backbite one another.** (Qur'an 49:12)

Openness and honest communication between husband and wife is absolutely essential in marriage and will always save from bitterness, suspicion and recrimination further down the line. When parents are open and forthright in their affairs and matters related with the family, it has a tremendous positive effect on the children. Children can easily relate to them, open their minds to them and discuss issues of importance. Openness may occasionally put parents on the spot, but this is how it should be. It gives more confidence to the children and in return makes the parents more self-aware. If parents happen to possess some undesirable habits or are inclined to some wrong practices they must come up with a determined effort to stop them. Attempts to hide them may have serious negative consequences on the children's upbringing.

---

8. From *Stories: Good and True for Children,* Translated by Matina Wali Muhammad, Ta-Ha Publishers, London, 1994

Openness and transparency generate virtue in the family. The personal and family life of the Prophet Muhammad ﷺ was in the full light of history, which, as a role model, illuminates Muslim life. Muslims hate hypocrisy in personal and social life. A Muslim parent should never have double standards in his life, especially with his children.

> **O you who believe, why do you say what you do not do? It is deeply abhorrent to Allah that you say what you do not do.** (Qur'an 61:2-3)

3.2 A FAMILY ETHOS BASED ON VALUES

Establishment of an Islamic ethos in the house is the enviable asset of a Muslim family. It is the joint responsibility of both the father and the mother. Children growing up in a positive family and community environment have a strong anchor in life. They are generally positive contributors to society. Children, from their early years, need to be trained properly so that they become part of this learning process and can contribute to the family according to their age and maturity.

Islam has five unique pillars. The rites of prayer (*salah*) and fasting (*sawm*) are open and done publicly and when parents practise them consistently children will inevitably follow their lead from early childhood. Parents need to expend extra effort to involve their young ones in social work, charity and other humanitarian works. Children should be taught about the importance of *'Eid* festivals, *zakah* and *Hajj* so that they are ingrained in their minds as they grow. As most people are eligible to pay *zakah* and perform

Hajj, they should be purposefully discharged in a way that children learn this from the points of view of the *deen* and society, not just the physical act of discharging the duty but the spirit of it and the consequences. The two Muslim celebrations give Muslim children invaluable opportunities to learn the essence of enjoyment in communal activities. They come to understand the bonding between Muslims that should last throughout the year. It is also important to give children something exciting to celebrate that is uniquely Muslim so that they do not feel deprived of, for example, their school friends celebrating birthdays and Christmas. Children should be encouraged to take part in discussion on all these issues in a manner they understand. If the basic Islamic practices are carried out with real spirit at home they make a permanent impact on the children's personalities and future lives. They also create a dynamic and happy family environment.

Purification of the self (*tazkiyah*) and personal development are essential in a world where wrong action proliferates in society and stress tends to dominate our daily life. This needs continuous remembrance of Allah (*dhikr*) and steadfastness (*sabr*) (Qur'an 7:205, 33:41-42). It also needs high spirit of mind, unrelenting struggle and selfless efforts to serve humanity for the sake of Allah. Our success on earth depends on purifying our selves (Qur'an 91:9).

A dynamic Muslim family continually strives to raise the spiritual elevation as well as the worldly success of its members. But human beings' success in the world (*dunya*) and the Hereafter (*akhirah*) is fully dependent on Allah's blessing. No matter how professionally people plan and how hard they try, the result is with Allah. This is the spirit of *tawakkul* (reliance on Allah) which protects human beings from the agony of uncertainty and fear of failure.

Allah loves those who put their trust (rely) on Him.
(Qur'an 3:159).

In this context, *du'a* (supplication) to Allah is invaluable. If performed correctly and with sincerity, it fills the human heart with contentment, since Allah does answer the *du'a* in a time and manner that are in accordance with His wisdom. The Messenger of Allah ﷺ has taught Muslims how to supplicate for good things at every moment and in hard times. It is not in the nature of a Muslim to despair or be despondent.

> *Allah is angry with he who does not ask (anything) from Him.*
> (At-Tirmidhi)

> *Supplication is the spirit of worship.* (At-Tirmidhi)

Supplication for children by the parents and vice versa is pleasing to Allah and is rewarding psychologically. It produces joy in the mind and tranquillity in the heart. It creates love and respect for and loyalty to each other. In response to the special prayer of the Prophet Ibrahim ﷺ (Qur'an 2:129), Allah promised the advent of Prophet Muhammad ﷺ. The Qur'an and the books of *hadith* contain supplications that should be practised by all in the family.

> **Our Lord, give us joy in our spouses and children and make us a good example for those who have taqwa.**
> (Qur'an 25:74)

> **Lord, show mercy to them as they did in looking after me when I was little.** (Qur'an 17:23-24)

In one *hadith* there are said to be three supplications that are answered – there being no doubt about it; the supplication of the oppressed, the supplication of the traveller and the supplication of the parent for the child (Ibn Majah).

3.3 CHALLENGING THE IMPEDIMENTS

A close-knit family with an Islamic ethos and a positive learning environment has the most likelihood of guarding everyone from evil – the evils of greed, selfishness, laxity and lust that thrive so rapidly, like viruses, in permissive societies. They are the impediments in human beings' journey towards Allah.

And then there are the threats that are haunting most parents today, Muslims and non-Muslim alike. The black hole of social diseases, negative peer pressure etc, is causing mayhem in society. Children are being 'lost' in the sea of whims and desires, sensuality and promiscuity, in a moral maze and a spiritual void. School phobia, truancy and disaffection are now becoming common, particularly with secondary-school age children. This is giving rise to delinquency, gangs, drug and alcohol addiction, bullying and criminal activities in the inner cities in which most Muslims are concentrated. In the absence of role models, and with racial prejudice and religious discrimination, the lack of motivation and low self-esteem are thwarting the potential of many in the community. The sense of impotence in the midst of global injustice is making many fatalist.

The list of impediments is long. The challenge faced by parents is enormous. Raising children in this social climate is becoming more demanding and parents need always to be on their guard. In spite of all their efforts in keeping everything in order, things can go wrong and tension and emotion can rise in the family. Human relationships are complex and often sensitive. Difficulties in a family most often start with small arguments, for whatever reasons, between husband and wife or between a child and parent. Petty arguments can create tension leading to conflict and anger. If not contained in time, anger may pile up and, like fire, it can burn the fabric of relationships in the family. Fortunately, most people are resilient in coping with their emotions. Many are able to turn all these challenges into opportunities.

As children grow, parental expectations of them rise. Parents look for obedience, discipline and a good output from their sons and daughters in almost everything. When this is not delivered or not seen to be delivered by the children, parents become disappointed and upset. Some parents become paranoid in the very first instance. Strong words are expressed, perhaps loudly, and things go wrong. Strong emotions are part of human nature and not everyone can express themselves as well as they intend. Many forget that while emotions in the right place and in the right manner are essential, they can be dangerous in the wrong place and wrong manner. Uncontrolled anger in the family is the recipe for disaster.

Muslim parents who want to create a new generation of capable Muslims for civilisational change themselves need a high level of behavioural management before they can train their younger ones. Conflicts do occur among human beings, but we must know how to resolve them. They are essential ingredients of parenting skills.

**Those who spend in ease and adversity, those who
control their rage and pardon other people – Allah
loves the good-doers.** (Qur'an 3:134)

Allah's Messenger ﷺ *mentioned, "Some are swift to anger and swift
to cool down, the one characteristic making up for the other; some are
slow to anger and slow to cool down, the one characteristic making up
for the other; but the best of you are those who are slow to anger and
swift to cool down; and the worst of you are those who are swift to
anger and slow to cool down." He continued, "Beware of anger, for
it is a live coal in the heart of the descendants of Adam. Do you not
notice the swelling of the vein of his neck and the redness of his eyes?
So, when anyone experiences anything of that nature he should lie
down and cleave to the earth."* (At-Tirmidhi)

*He is not strong who throws down another, but he is [strong] who
control his anger.* (Sahih al-Bukhari and Muslim)

3.4 EXECUTIVE SUMMARY

- Happy and spiritually successful families with solid human
  and Islamic values stand the best chance of producing good
  human beings. However, the ultimate destiny belongs to
  Allah. A solid family can bring a sense of belonging, anchor
  and roots and build balanced beings in children, who can
  then contribute to society. Children growing up in these
  families are best equipped with the necessary tools to create
  blessed societies.

- There are some essential ingredients necessary to make up a
  happy and blessed family, such as love, mercy, respect, loyalty,

forgiveness, sacrifice, fairness, honesty and openness. Their absence from any family or society is disastrous. In the midst of injustice, oppression and vengeance, the world cannot afford the weakening of the institution of the family.

• In addition, Muslim families should be reservoirs of knowledge and learning. Islamic principles and the acts of worship should be openly practised so that children can simply make them their life habits. The family environment should carry a positive message and leave an imprint of the Islamic ethos.

• The family environment should be free of dry and lifeless practices. A lively and open environment with freedom of thought produces confidence in children who do not feel any inhibition in expressing themselves and acting proactively.

• Muslims have to watch out for pitfalls, so that no one in the family falls through the net. Supplication for children by parents and vice-versa is pleasing to Allah and is psychologically rewarding. It blends the relationship between them and creates love for each other.

• Muslim families should be at the heart of wider society - sharing happiness, concerns and aspirations with not only fellow Muslims but also with all those around them. Human beings have a common destiny when it comes to safety, fairness, justice and maintaining an ecological balance on earth.

Conclusion

Human beings crave hope and success. They need them in their personal lives, in their families and in their communities. The search for a sense of fulfilment drives people forward. For Muslims and many people in the world today, a successful marriage leading to successful families and right-acting children is a very important part of life. Human beings cannot remain loners; they need friends, spouses and partners to share their thoughts, ideas, experiences, joys and pains. Allah created a partner for the first man so that, as husband and wife, they could live in peace and tranquillity. When they came down to earth they formed the first human family and fulfilled the divine requirement of sowing the seeds of humankind. From these two people in the beginning, there are now over six billion human beings on earth, the diverse human race.

Marriage and family should thus be treated seriously. While marriage is a legal contract between two responsible adults, the family is a part of the bedrock of human society. Neither marriage nor families can be taken casually. To Muslims they are an integral part of their *deen*. No matter in what age or land, they have universal importance.

Building a sound Muslim family is important for most Muslim men and women. Parenting as an endeavour for the greater good of humanity can only succeed in positive family environments. Muslim parents in modern societies, given the prevalent socio-cultural and moral conditions, obviously have a most challenging task. The starting point is the understanding of the challenge and then following in the footsteps of the early Muslims in the present context. Here comes the primordial importance of good conduct and behaviour in the family. The prophets were sent to teach humanity good conduct and right behaviour. By being the role model in all aspects of family life the last Prophet ﷺ emphasised its importance eloquently,

> *The best of you is the best to his family and I am the best among you to my family.* (Ibn Majah)

> *The most perfect believers are the best in conduct, and the best of you are those who are best to their spouses.* (At-Tirmidhi)

As mentioned, husbands are generally the breadwinners in a family. However, for genuine economic and professional reasons wives in a family may desire to work. They may wish to give a helping hand in earning for the family, although they have no legal obligation to do so. However, this must not be compromised with the Islamic upbringing and education of children. There should be open and frank discussion and consultation between the spouses for the overall welfare of the family. Children, being at the centre of any planning and action, should be involved as and when necessary, according to their age and maturity. This is important for inculcating in them the sense of responsibility and making them aware of the realities of life.

Families can be life-long schools for human beings. Muslim families are centres of learning if the environment is healthy and positive. The family of the Prophet Muhammad ﷺ, with his measured, lively and meaningful dealings with family members, remains the role model for humanity. There was liveliness without vulgarity, seriousness without tension and competition in *taqwa* without rivalry. It was the reservoir of knowledge and virtue from which the Companions ﷺ quenched their thirst for knowledge of the conduct of an ideal family.

Life is full of serious and complex issues, but to make it meaningful our body and spirit need space for humour and enjoyment. Both husband and wife should strive to give their partner the joys and pleasures of life. The Messenger of Allah ﷺ used to cut lively, but innocent, jokes with his wives. He ran races with his young wife, *Umm al-Mu'minin* A'ishah ﷺ. One day he defeated her and said that it was in revenge for his defeat in the previous race! The *hadith*, "Entertain the hearts in between hours, for if the hearts become tired they become blind" (Sunan al-Daylami), is a glowing lesson for us. Lively encounters and a sense of humour bring people closer. Khalif Umar ﷺ used to advise his people that when men are in their houses with their wives they should behave in a relaxed manner. This insistence on a stress-free life does not mean that a Muslim family loses seriousness when gravity is necessary.

Virtue proliferates in a right-acting family where husband and wife lead a purposeful and happy life. They protect each other and together they protect children in the family. Everyone contributes to the happy atmosphere. Blessed families contribute to a blessed society and ultimately lead toward an *ummah* of purpose. This is a virtuous cycle. In a sound and responsible family no one can fall through the net. Everyone watches out so that no one becomes lost. Parents and children pray for each other. The maxim, 'the family that prays together stays together', becomes meaningful.

And the believers, men and women, are protecting friends of one another; they enjoin the right and forbid the wrong, and they establish prayer and they pay the poor-due, and they obey Allah and His Messenger. As for these, Allah will have mercy on them. Verily, Allah is Mighty, Wise. (Qur'an 9:71)

The threat to marriage and the family institution comes from human beings' refusal to accept the supremacy of their Lord in their lives. Their arrogant refusal to become slaves of one Lord makes them slaves of their own whims and desires. Marriage and family do not fit with their egos because they entail rights, responsibility and accountability. They want to enjoy life with unrestrained freedom, no matter whether that harms their long-term future, or their partners and their offspring. This is the age in which we live now. This is the age of the moral maze and spiritual void, the age of proselytising materialism.

The fruits of an irreligious lifestyle are having their toll. The ill effects of cohabitation and rampant extramarital sex are teenage pregnancy, single-parent families, family disintegration, domestic violence and the rise in the number of 'problem' children. All these are eating away at the fabric of community harmony and social stability. It is now costing developed countries economically and socially, leading to gloomy national futures. Human beings are losing their mutual trust, mental peace and the purpose of life.

The trend of individualism, consumerism, egoism, uncontrolled promiscuity and sensuality is on the rise. For any society and nation all these can have devastating consequences.

Muslims in modern societies cannot afford to ignore these issues. In a globalised world, particularly in the West, they are gradually becoming vulnerable to this social trend. The shockwaves of these social diseases are having negative effects in their families and communities and already there are signs of cracks in Muslim families. There are signs of confusion among Muslim youth about their identity and this is manifested in poor performance in society at large. Unless addressed with a sense of urgency, things can only become more difficult in years to come.

Marriage and family are the pillars of a stable society and nation. Our success in this world and the Hereafter depends on how we perform as the emissaries of Allah on earth. Marriage gives us solace and tranquillity of mind and heart. Family gives us an anchor. The love, affection, warmth and emotional attachment created between a man and a woman thrive in marriage and family bonding and are transmitted to our offspring. Together they become the strongest unit, the fortress, of the human race. As such, marriage and family are absolutely vital for human beings to succeed.

It is our duty, therefore, to fulfil our obligations with regards to marriage and families as Allah intended and has prescribed for us in Islam. Only then can we expect to be successful and contented as individuals and as an *ummah* both in this world and the Hereafter, insha'Allah.

Glossary of Islamic Terms

Adab   Good manners, etiquette, custom. In Islam it has ethical and social implications. It includes the meaning of civility, courtesy and refinement.

'Adl   Justice, fairness, equilibrium and equity. A fundamental value governing social behaviour, dealings and the legal framework.

Allah   Creator and Sustainer of all. This Arabic word is unique. It has no feminine and no plural. No other word, in any language, carries the meaning of 'Allah'.

Ahl al-Kitab People of the Book, i.e. those people who received an authentic revelation before Islam, meaning the Jews and Christians. The judgement has been extended to some degree to other religions. People of the Book may live under the governance of Islam by their own revelations and laws, under certain conditions.

Akhirah   Hereafter. The Day of Judgement and the Life after Death. One of the articles of faith in Islam.

'alaihi's-salam (ﷺ)

> Peace be upon him. Mentioned after the name of a Prophet.

Amir
> Leader, lit. 'commander'. A term applied both to the Khalif and to subsidiary and other leaders in general.

'Asabiyah
> Tribal loyalty and the whole complex of relationships to be found in natural peoples because of their kin structures. When people put it and the needs of their group or clan ahead of the deen of Allah and the needs of the whole community it becomes a blameworthy concept.

Ayat (sing. ayah)

> Verses of the Qur'an. It literally means a sign or an indication, and also means a miracle.

Barakah
> Blessing, any good that is bestowed by Allah and especially that which increases.

Deen
> The life-transaction. More than 'religion' since it encompasses all aspects of life including buying and selling, and the governance of the Muslims.

Dhikr
> Remembrance or mention of Allah.

Du'a
> Supplication to Allah.

Dunya
> The present world. It stems from a root which means lower or nearer.

'Eid
> Celebration. 'Eid al-Fitr is the celebration upon conclusion of the month of fasting and 'Eid al-Adha is the celebration of sacrifice upon conclusion of the Hajj.

Fiqh　　　　Islamic jurisprudence, from a verb which means 'to understand'.

Hadith (pl. *Ahadith*)
　　　　　Literally, an account. Accounts of the sayings, deeds and tacit approvals of the Messenger of Allah ﷺ.

Hajj　　　　Pilgrimage. Once in a lifetime journey of a physically and economically capable adult Muslim to Makkah; the fifth pillar of Islam. Elements in it stem from the time of Adam عليه السلام, and from the sacrifice of the Prophet Ibrahim عليه السلام.

Halal　　　　Permissible. Lawful. Anything permitted by Islamic *Shari'ah*.

Haram　　　Unlawful. Anything prohibited by the *Shari'ah*.

'Ibadah　　　Worship, obedience to Allah.

Ijab　　　　Refers to the 'offer' part of a contract.

Imam　　　Today it means a person who leads congregational prayers. Also a reputable scholar but, in its original meaning, the leader of the Muslim community.

Iman　　　　Belief in and affirmation of the articles of faith enunciated in the Qur'an and the Sunnah, i.e. belief in Allah, His Messengers, His Books, His angels, the Last Day and that the Decree of good and evil is from Him. *Iman*, which can increase or decrease, is the doorway to Islam.

Islam　　　　Literally to submit and to offer peace. Life transaction (see *Deen*) of submission to the will of Allah, expounded by all the prophets.

Istikharah	Special prayer intended to ask for an indication or guidance from Allah when taking a difficult decision as to which choice is likely to be of benefit.
Jahiliyah	Ignorance (of divine guidance). Refers to the later part of the period between Prophet 'Isa ﷺ and the Messenger of Allah ﷺ when people forgot the teachings of the prophets.
Khalif	The leader of the Muslim *ummah*.
Khul'	The process through which a Muslim woman obtains a divorce from her husband through an Islamic court. If a Muslim woman finds that she is simply incompatible with her husband, she may offer to return some or all of her dower (*mahr*) or in some other manner to compensate him, and thus obtain a divorce.
Khutbah an-Nikah	The sermon delivered at the time of the *Nikah*.
Kufu'	Compatibility or suitability (between marriage partners).
Libas	Garment (as mentioned in the Qur'an 2:187 to describe the relationship between husband and wife).
Mahr	Dower, a compulsory due (cash or kind) to a bride from the groom according to the groom's financial ability. It may be *muajjal* (paid at the time) or *muakhkhar* (deferred).

Mahram Relation with whom marriage is forbidden. *Ghair Mahram* is someone who does not fall into the category of *Mahram*.

Muslim A believer who willingly submits to Allah alone and practises Islam.

Nikah Marriage according to a simple Islamic contract.

Qist Similar to *'Adl*. Justice, fairness, equilibrium and equity. A fundamental value governing social behaviour, dealings and legal framework.

Qubul Acceptance in a contract.

Qur'an The final Book and revelation from Allah to humankind, revealed to the Prophet Muhammad ﷺ over a span of twenty-three years.

Radi'Allahu 'anha (﵂)

May Allah be pleased with her. Mentioned after the name of a female Companion or member of the family of the Prophet Muhammad ﷺ.

Radi'Allahu 'anhu (﵁)

May Allah be pleased with him. Mentioned after the name of a male Companion of the Prophet Muhammad ﷺ.

Radi'Allahu 'anhum (﵃)

May Allah be pleased with them.

Rahmah Mercy (of Allah).

Sabr	Steadfastness. The word has a wider and more positive meaning in Islam than simply patient endurance of suffering.
Sahih	Literally 'sound'. A *hadith* whose chain of narrators are each authentic in their beliefs, characters, scholarship and memories and who each have received it directly from the previous such narrator in the chain of transmission which connects directly back to the Messenger of Allah ﷺ. Higher than it in status is the *Mutawatir hadith* which is transmitted by so many different chains of narration that there can be no possible doubt about its authenticity.
Sakinah	Tranquillity and peace of mind that comes due to the blessings of Allah.
Salah	The prayer, particularly the five times daily ritual prayer which is compulsory as the second pillar of Islam.

Sallallahu alaihi wa sallam (ﷺ)

Peace and blessings be upon him. Mentioned after the name of the Prophet Muhammad ﷺ.

Sawm	Fasting, particularly, the compulsory month-long fast during the month of Ramadan, which is the fourth pillar of Islam.
Shari'ah	Derived from a word meaning 'a road' particularly one leading to water in the desert. Used to mean Islam's legal system and the rules by which Muslims abide.

Shaheed	A martyr who dies for the sake of Allah in the way of Islam.
Sunnah	Literally, a custom or practice. The body of practices of the Prophet Muhammad ﷺ. It also includes the practice established by the rightly guided first four Khalifs. It is sometimes mistakenly assumed to be synonymous with *hadith*.
Surah	Chapter of the Qur'an. There are 114 *surahs*, some of which are very long and others short.
Talaq	Divorce initiated by men, according to the strict *Shari'ah* requirements.
Taqwa	Fear or consciousness of Allah that leads to abandonment of wrong action and embodiment of right action. It is both an inner feeling of a human being towards the Creator and the effects of that upon his actions.
Tawakkul	Reliance on Allah, which gives mental tranquillity and peace of mind.
Tazkiyah	Purification or growth, in the moral or ethical sense in order to purge from the soul base qualities and desires.
'Ulama	People of knowledge. The term has wrongly become confined to religious scholars.
Ummah	Community of believers worldwide, irrespective of race, colour, language or geographical boundary. The universal body of Muslims as a single community,

properly when living by the *Shari'ah* and living under the governance of Islamic rulers.

Umm al-Mu'minin
    Mother of the believers (a name for each of the Prophet Muhammad's ﷺ wives)

'Umrah   Lesser pilgrimage to Makkah with specific rites.

Wali   Legal guardian.

Walima   The marriage banquet which is given by the groom following the consummation of the marriage.

Zakah   The compulsory yearly due payable by a wealthy Muslim, as a part of his obligation, mainly for the benefit of the poor and the needy; the third pillar of Islam. This pillar is wrongly thought to be an act of personal charity left to the conscious of the individual Muslim.

Zina   Unlawful sexual intercourse, adultery, fornication.

Bibliography

Akhtar, Shabbir (1993) *The Muslim Parents Handbook: What Every Muslim Parent Should Know,* Ta-Ha Publishers, London

Al-Albani, Muhammad Naasiruddeen (1998) *The Etiquettes of Marriage: In the Pure Tradition of the Prophet,* Ihyaa' Minhaaj Al-Sunnah, UK

Al-Areefee, Yoosuf ibn Abdullah (1996) *Manners of Welcoming the Newborn Child in Islam,* Maktaba Darus Salaam, UK

Al-Bukhari, Imam, *Sahih al-Bukhari,* Translated by Dr. Muhammad Muhsin Khan (1997), Darussalam, Riyadh.

Al-Ghazali, M (1989) *Muslim Character,* IIFSO

Al-Ghazali, (1991) *Ihya Ulum-ud-din, Book II,* New Delhi

Al-Kaysi, Marwan I (1994) *Morals and Manners in Islam: A Guide to Islamic Adab,* The Islamic Foundation, UK

Altalib, Hisham, (1993) *Training Guide for Islamic Workers.* Herndon, VA: IIIT and IIFSO

Ali Nadwi, Abul Hasan (1983) *Islam and the World,* IIFSO

An-Nawawi, Imam, *Riyad-us-Saleheen,* (1998) Islamic Book Service, Delhi

Asad, Muhammad (1980) *The Message of the Qur'an,* Dar al-Andalus Ltd, Gibraltar

Azami, Iqbal A (1990) *Muslim Manners,* UK Islamic Academy, UK

Bashier, Zakaria (1991) *The Makkan Crucible,* The Islamic Foundation, Leicester

Bashier, Zakaria (1998) *Sunshine at Madinah,* The Islamic Foundation, Leicester

Beshir, Ekram and Mohamed Rida, (1998) *Meeting the Challenge of Parenting in the West: An Islamic Perspective.* Amanah Publications, USA

Bewley, Abdalhaqq and Aisha (1999) *The Noble Qur'an: A New Rendering of its Meaning in English,* Bookwork, Norwich

Campion, Mukti J (1993) *The Good Parent Guide,* Element, UK

Doi, Abdur Rahman I, (1989) *Woman in Shariah,* Ta-Ha Publishers, London

D'Oyen, Fatima M (1996) *The Miracle of Life: A Guide on Islamic Family Life and Sex Education for Young People,* The Islamic Foundation, Leicester

Eyre, Linda and Richard, (1980) *Teaching Your Children Joy,* Fireside, New York

Eyre, Linda and Richard, (1993) *Teaching Your Children Values,* Fireside, New York

Eyre, Linda and Richard, (1994) *Teaching Your Children Responsibility,* Fireside, New York

Fenwick, Elizabeth and Smith, Dr. Tony, (1994) *Adolescence – The Survival Guide for Parents and Teenagers,* London

Gaffney, Maureen, et al, (1991) *Parenting: A Handbook for Parents,* Town House, UK

Hamid, Abdul Wahid (1995) *Companions of the Prophet,* MELS, Leicester

Haralambos and Holborn Sociology, (1995, 4th Ed) *Sociology: Themes and Perspectives,* Harper Collins, London

Hammudah Abd al-Ati, (1977) *The Family Structure in Islam,* American Trust Publication, Indianapolis, USA

Hasan, Suhaib (1998) *Raising Children in Islam,* Al-Qur'an Society, London

Haykal, M. H. (1976) *The Life of Muhammad (saas),* American Trust Publication, Indianapolis, USA

Huda al-Khattab, (1997) *Bent Rib: A Journey Through Women's Issue in Islam,* Ta-Ha Publishers, London

Joslin, Karen R, (1994) *The Parent's Problem Solver: Practical Solutions to over 140 Childhood problems,* Vermilion, London

Klein Mavis and Piatkus Judy, (1991) *Understanding Your Child: An A-Z for Parents,* Piatkus Ltd, London

Lang, Jeffrey (1997) Even Angels Ask – *A Journey to Islam in America,* Amana Publications, USA

Lang, Jeffrey (1994) *Struggling to Surrender,* Amana Publications, USA

Lemu, Aisha and Hereen, Fatima (1978) *Women in Islam,* The Islamic Foundation, Leicester

Maqsood, Ruqaiyyah Waris (1995) *Living with Teenagers: A Guide for Muslim Parents,* Ta-Ha Publishers, London

Maudoodi, Sayyid, Abul A'la (1982) *Let us be Muslims,* Edited by Khurram Murad, The Islamic Foundation, Leicester

Maudoodi, Sayyid, Abul A'la (1995) *Towards Understanding Islam,* The Islamic Foundation, Leicester

Murad, Khurram (2000) *In the Early Hours: Reflections on Spiritual and Self Development,* Revival Publications, UK

Muslim, Imam, *Sahih Muslim,* Translated by Abdul Hamid Siddiqi (1990) Ashraf Islamic Publishers, Lahore

Muslim Students' Association, (1976) *Parents' Manual: A Guide for Muslim Parents Living in North America,* American Trust Publications, USA

Pickthall, Muhammad Marmaduke, *The Meaning of the Glorious Qur'an: Text and Explanatory Translation,* New American Library

Rahman, Afzalur (1986) *Role of Muslim Woman in Society,* Seerah Foundation, London

Sabiq, As-Sayyid (1404AH) *Fiqh-us-Sunnah,* Dar El Fateh for Arab Information, Plainfield, Indiana

Sarwar, G (1996) *Sex Education: The Muslim Perspective,* The Muslim Educational Trust, London

At-Tirmidhi, Imam, *Shama'il Tirmidhi* (2001) Darul Ishaat, Karachi

Wali Muhammad, Matina (1994) *Stories: Good and True for Children* (translated), Ta-Ha Publishers, London

Yusuf Ali, Abdullah (1997) *The Holy Qur'an,* Islamic Book Service, Delhi